QUEER ARAB MARTYR

JAD JABER

ATROPOS PRESS
new york • dresden

QUEER ARAB MARTYR

THE HAREM OF QUEER SECRETS

Jad Jaber

Atropos Press

Think Media EGS Series is supported by the European Graduate School

ATROPOS PRESS
New York • Dresden

151 First Avenue # 14, New York, N.Y. 10003

Book Design and Illustration by Diaa Mrad based on original Jad Jaber paintings

I-S-B-N 978-1-940813-37-0

Contents

CHAPTER ONE: QUEER IN THE LAND OF SODOM   2

CHAPTER TWO: THE ART OF TIMID NEGOTIATIONS   10

CHAPTER THREE: THE VIRTUOUS QUEER ARAB   20

CHAPTER FOUR: THE QUEER ARAB SHAKRA   32

CHAPTER FIVE: THE QUEER EXISTENTIALIST   44

CHAPTER SIX: THE PHENOMENAL EVENT OF ARAB QUEERNESS 56

CHAPTER SEVEN: ATTENTION TO INTENTION   64

CHAPTER EIGHT: QUEER ARAB TONGUE   74

CHAPTER NINE: "I QUEER, THEREFOR I AM"   80

CHAPTER TEN: QUEER PUBLIC SECRETS   90

CHAPTER ELEVEN: QUEER MIGRATION   98

CHAPTER TWELVE: THE QUEER GYM ETHNOGRAPHY   110

CHAPTER THIRTEEN: VIOLENT QUEER RELATION-ING   116

CHAPTER FOURTEEN: ICKY, STICKY QUEER SEX   122

CHAPTER FIFTEEN: ARAB QUEER METAMORPHOSIS   128

CHAPTER SIXTEEN: IT'S A QUEER WAR   140

CHAPTER SEVENTEEN: TIME TO PAUSE   148

CHAPTER EIGHTEEN: QUEER WAR SEMIOTICS   154

CHAPTER NINETEEN: FEAR OF THE QUEER NEIGHBOR   162

CHAPTER TWENTY: NO QUEER IS AN ISLAND   170

CHAPTER ONE

Queer in the Land of Sodom

The deep understanding of queerness in the Arab world[i] is as *vague* and *convoluted* as *queerness* is in the Arab world. An emotional, philosophical and psychosocial understanding of queerness *requires* a name, a place and an identity. It requires a holistic subject. It requires a queer martyr[ii].

CAN YOU EXIST PUBLICALLY AS QUEER IN THE ARAB WORLD?

What do you have to martyr with to be a queer Arab?

WHAT ARE ARAB YOUTH'S FIRST QUEER EXPERIENCES?

WHAT ARE ARAB "COMING-OUT" EXPERIENCES LIKE?

When was the last time an Arab mother proudly identified her child as queer?

HOW IS IT LIKE TO GROW UP QUEER, ARAB AND IN WAR?

i   Arab World: Egypt, Iraq, Saudi Arabia, Yemen, Qatar, United Arab Emirates, Lebanon, Syria, Jordan, Palestine, Kuwait and Oman.
ii Martyring used to mean witnessing. Enough people died witnessing truth that the meaning became "to die for the truth/cause"

HAVE ARABS ALWAYS HAD AN ANTI-QUEER STANCE?

What are the terms of consummating queer love in the Arab world?

CAN AN ARAB QUEER FREELY DREAM WHEN IT IS BUSY SURVIVING?

"I sometimes have this recurrent dream and I wake up heaving. I read my name, K.Y, in the morning news and it says: "K.Y, found in apartment in North Lebanon, engaging in unnatural and queer behavior". My dream goes further to get a call from my mom. That is what usually wakes me up screaming"

-Kareem, 25, Lebanon

The queer context in Lebanon can *best* be described with the recent anti-homophobia campaigns and venues that have refused to host queer events. "A hotel in Beirut serving as a venue for Beirut Pride canceled before the event because of security threats. A series of crackdowns on gay-friendly nightclubs, bathhouses and events has stirred sizable debate in the national media."[iii]

ARAB *SPACES* ARE RELUCTANT TO HOST QUEER BODIES AS ARAB *BODIES* ARE RELUCTANT TO HOST QUEERNESS. As it appears, the *contested* space of the Arab queer is that of *constant* negotiations and sometimes, violence.

iii   https://www.oroom.org/forum/threads/beirut-gay-pride-2017.52341/

This dynamic is *also* part of the queer Arab body, a venue that has been met with externalized *and* internalized protests. The fact that the queer subject is becoming more of a public secret and more *hidden in the open* indicates changes in Arab culture that *resistance to queer existence* may be weakening. Recently, a series of Lebanese judges ruled against treating homosexuality as a crime in court hearings and the Lebanese Psychiatric Society called for the abolition of the law that describes homosexual sex as unnatural and illegal.

The queer's *negotiated* subjectivity in the Arab context might be described as *more* complex than just *a benign growth on the sovereign Arab body*. But *how* much is this negotiation *really* causing change and making way for "an event"? The Arab queer is currently attempting to establish a political, creative, cultural and economic identity, as queer *and* Arab, a process that usually includes a *struggle* for this marginalized community.

Everything in the unconscious seeks outward manifestation and the (queer) personality *too* desires to evolve *out* of its unconscious conditions and to experience itself as a whole (Jung, 1936)

"To create intenionally and consciously using various mediums is the ultimate act of freedom, resistance and revolution. There is an abundance of Arab queer art at this point in history. It just needs more visibility"

- Bshara, 30, Lebanese-Syrian

There is nothing new *in* the struggle of the marginalized.

There *is* something new in the struggle *in* the Arab world that *simultaneously* prohibits *and* fetishizes queerness.

There *is* something new in negotiating queer meaning behind Arab *male-to-male* closeness, embedded in daily gendered *spaces* and *rituals*.

THERE IS SOMETHING NEW, SOMETHING OLD, SOMETHING BURROWED AND SOMETHING BLUE IN ARAB QUEERNESS.

The recent pride event in Lebanon could have broken significant ground, just as a recent online and television advertisement did by featuring a lesbian couple. One of Lebanon's oldest and largest restaurant chains commissioned the ad, a first for Lebanese advertising, "to include people we see everywhere around us," the ad stated.(Orange room, 2017).

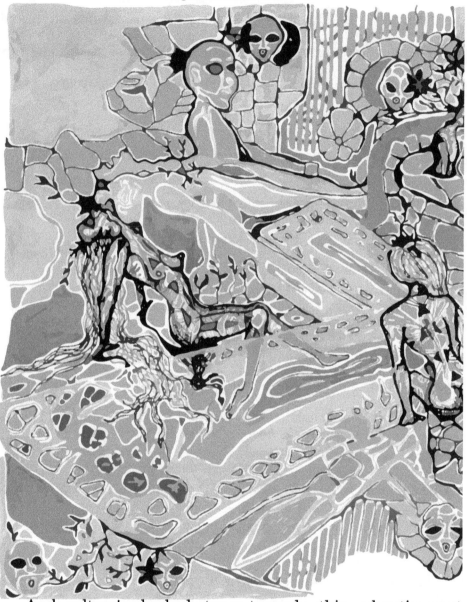

Arab culture's shocked stance towards this advertisement was shocking in *itself*. After all, as the article above mentioned, queers are people that "we see everwhere" in the Arab world. Of course, you can *see* them, as long as you do not *label* them and as long as *they* do not label *themselves* as queer.

Faber, Jad. Rite of Passage, 2006

These invisible queers are the paradox of the Arab archetype, the *familiar stranger*, the neighbor whose name cannot be remembered. The people you *know* are queer, but cannot *say* are queer. The problem is that the space of the *familiar stranger* does not leave much chance for the *growth* of a whole queer subject who needs to be *known*, *represented* and *accepted* for self-development.

9

2

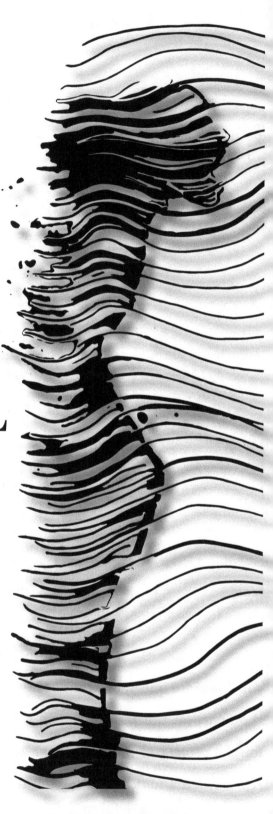

Faber, Fad. Bodies of Resistance, 2009

A MANUAL

ON HOW

TO

SCREAM,

Silently

CHAPTER TWO

Timid Queer Negotiations:
A Manual on How to Scream, Silently

"Beirut Pride is not looking to promote legal rights like gay marriage, nor do organizers seek to repeal the penal code that prohibits sexual acts contrary to the order of nature. It is simply seeking to banalize LGBT people, to help "transcend labels" that alienate individuals of certain sexual identities."

- Pride Activist, (Orange room, May 2017).

The negotiation above attempts to *lighten* the seriousness of queer issues by attempting to "transcend labels" which is another meaning for "*erasing* labels".

In an act of "activism", advocates for queer subjects, such as the pride activist quoted above, erase and downplay the *impact* of their own label. In the mean time, Arab heteronormative culture suppresses *everything* that behaves outside its required guidelines. This is an example of the *containment* of queerness by both its advocates and critics.

What would have happened with a queer *spillover*?

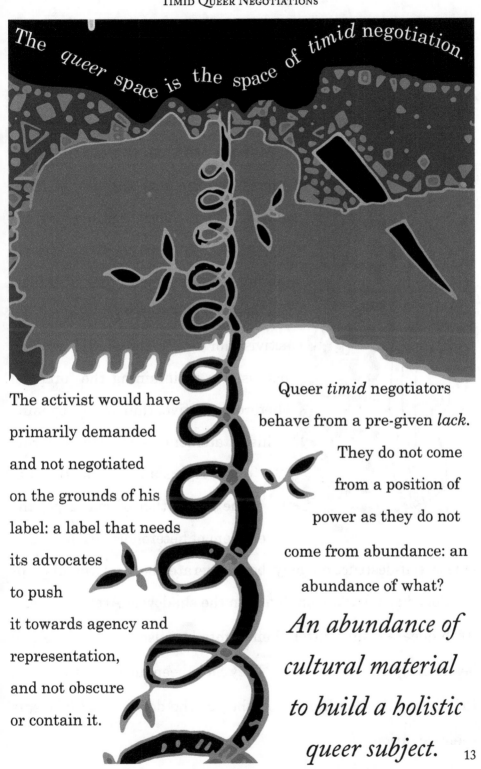

The queer space is the space of *timid* negotiation.

The activist would have primarily demanded and not negotiated on the grounds of his label: a label that needs its advocates to push it towards agency and representation, and not obscure or contain it.

Queer *timid* negotiators behave from a pre-given *lack*. They do not come from a position of power as they do not come from abundance: an abundance of what?

An abundance of cultural material to build a holistic queer subject.

13

Already setting their weapons aside, Arab queers give up their inalienable rights to be simply a *part* of nature, *not* "contrary" to its order. The queer negotiates and does *not* demand because it *believes* in society's Order of Things (Foucault, 1966).

Queers are the real *martyrs* of Arab society. The queer self-martyrs as often as society martyrs it to actively maintain the imagined order of things. The pride activist before was not an activist for queer rights. He was an activist for maintaining the "order of heteronormative things" by opening his statement with surrendering queer rights and "not disturbing" the institution of marriage, the emblem of heteronormativity.

Queer self-destruction may be deliberate, born of impulse, *or* developed as a habit from living in the shadow of Arab culture. Arab queers cannot utter their rights because their tongue had been *cut off* at its fetal stage. They have been nurtured to believe that either the death of *their* label, or the death of *all* labels, is their salvation.

14

Labels *should not* be killed...

Labels *should* be re-tagged...

Re-tagged on the queer Arab subject *alongside* the labels of "social worker, father, educator", "nurse, mother, bread-earner" and "friend, family, partner". *This* form of activism represents labels *with subjects* as individuals with faces, names, professions, dreams, emotions and rights *irreducible* to "unnatural" queer *objects*.

The space for existing, *but* not publically...

Of speaking, *but* not offending...

Of rebelling and yelling, *but* in whispers...

Of negotiating labels *but* relinquishing rights... is that of *existing* in the shadows, and *never* leaving the cave.

Arab queers constantly negotiate their identity with their culture. They mirror its disdain and rejection. Symptoms of the ongoing negotiations include habits of self-destruction and chronic anxiety: The anxious queer phallus.

The advertisement described in page 7, featuring a *lesbian* couple, begged the question: Was gay too much to handle for Arab culture? Is it more acceptable to represent *feminized* lesbians as a form of Arab *and* queer, but not gay? That would frame the *context* of a culture that glamorizes, yet stigmatizes *forms* of femininity. Yes, to feminine-looking lesbians, No to feminine-looking gays. This is a culture built on the male gaze. A culture whose men are comfortable publically stating that they "want a whore in bed *and* a virgin to the world". A culture that prohibits *and* seeks "secret pleasures" like the ever-expansive sexual market for transsexuals in the gulf and Lebanon. A culture with more "harems" than *you* can count.

Faber, Fad. The Self Preening, 2003

Had Arab culture appreciated "outright" pleasure and "outright" sexualities, there would not be a *need* for the constant negotiation of queer spaces and subjectivities.

But *we* Arabs like to dig before finding the bone. We enjoy the

slave's pleasure in

the blind eye

of the Master,

and we enjoy

negotiating

for it.

More recently,

Threats from

religious figures

forcibly

Jaber, Jad. The Self–Fucker 1996

cancelled an LGBTQ rights event. The Association of Muslim

Scholars labeled the event a crime against virtue and

threatened with mobilising "all those who care about virtue and

honor" against the queer cause.

18

The conference *No matter who they love, they remain my children* encouraged family support for LGTBQ children.

This can go down on the list of other "cancelled events" in the name of Arab virtue...Cancelled love when its nature is not hetrosexual...Cancelled sexualities when they do not fall within the bounds of marriage...Cancelled education when it does not fall within the bounds of religion...All events, including the salvific event of queer love, are under the threat of cancelation when they do not abide by Arab virtue.

3

THE VIRTUOUS QUEER

ARAB

Chapter Three

The Virtuous Queer Arab

"Virtue *versus* vice" embedded in Arab culture and its Abrahamic religions does not translate *directly* into "heteronormative *versus* queer", as an essentialist, reductionist or orientalist might perceive it. The sexual dynamics of the Arab world are *more* complex, embedded in a process of negotiation, and the need of "Arab pleasure" to be constantly "harem-ed"[iv] and "haram"[v]-ed.

> *I often travel from Dubai to Riyadh to go to these wild parties in super private and lavish spaces, usually separate from the family home. As long as you know someone local with power, you can do whatever you want in the Gulf. Dubai seems more gay friendly on the outside, but there is actually more control. It is more anti-queer."*

- Amir, 31, United Arab Emirates

iv   *Harem*, Arabic, a seperate and private part of a muslim household reserved for wives, concubines and female servants.
v   *Haram*, Arabic, a subject or object that is prohibited, immoral, and against cultural norms: for example, it is Haram to be queer in the Arab world.

Notice that the similarity of these Arabic words, "Harem", "Haram" and "Hareem[vi]" is not *just* for the confusing effect of its semantics. The *spaces* and *subjects* of these words *are* confusing in real-life, depicting "hidden pleasure hubs" and acts of exoticism, eroticism and fetishism associated with the *real* Arab orgasm, or **"little death"**. The intensity for little Arab deaths to occur lies in the fleeting hidden nature of "Haram" acts and "Harem-ed" spaces. Queers *can* queer in *these* pleasure hubs. Bodies *can* move, hair *can* be unveiled, language *can* reveal, and vice *can* become virtue.

"El-Mahjoub, Marghoub[vii]"

-Ahmad, 27. Syrian

Imbedded in its rigorous institutional and cultural affirmation to virtue, Arab culture was unknowingly cultivating vice. In addition, imbedded in what Arab culture might tag as vice, is the *ultimate* virtue...The queer living in truth.

"Arab sex is dirty sex, and in a good way. I come here from London for the sex. Arab men have more passion for it."

-Housam, 27, Iraq, on coming back to Lebanon, Syria and Jordan to explore queer Arab sex.

---

vi   Hareem, noun, plural, Arabic, meaning women.
vii An arabic proverb translating to "That which is veiled is also wanted"

Truth and virtue cannot be equal in a culture that primarily rewards virtue. An example of that would be women being seen as "virgin objects" versus "sexualized subjects".

"Islam is obsessed with Virginity. Even after we die, Islam says we get 72 virgins in paradise if, off-course, we are moral and straight"

-Azzem, 23, Qatar

The virgin Arab woman has no sexual history. Her body is untouched. She is wired to serve *one* man after marriage, wired to manage a home, and wired to bear children. That is the virtuous life that she is rewarded for by her god and culture.

Jaber, Jad. The Godless Priest. 2005

"My first relationship was abusive. It was with a particularly pious Arab man. My second was with a man from a similar background. I struggled with the abuse as a 17-year old girl, silently. Had I said anything, they would have called me a whore. Had I had more relationships with men like him, I would have been more abused silently. As an Arab women, I have the right to say: they are mysogynist. No one else can say it, but an Arab woman. Context is everything. We are entitled to call them for what they are because we lived it. The problem is that there are not enough Arab women calling them for what they are."

- Judy, 29, Lebanese

Arab women martyr their truth and essence on a daily basis for their social survival, as do Arab queers. During my extensive interviews with queer youth, the matriarchs of the family household and other female figures such as the mother, aunt or niece, inflicted a sizeble portion of the reported cultural violence that queers experienced. The reason being is that Arab women rear their children closely and for the *longest* time possible.   25

Arab women feel a heavier emotional responsibility for the outcome of their children and culture is more likely to pinpoint the failure of the youth/children back to the women of the household, rather than the men.

It is a shame that Arab women and queers are not comrades in the war against heteronormativity because they have both paid a large price to fit into that strict mold that Arab culture created for them.

The history for Arab queerness has been one of a collective, *selective amnesia*, and a modern present of *queer cleansing*.

"A protest was held in the Lebanese capital Beirut against the use of anal tests on men suspected of homosexuality, a criminal offence in the Arab countries" (Press 2000).

The protest came after the police raided a queer venue in the working class district of Beirut where thirty-six men were arrested, taken into custody and forced to undergo anal tests to determine their sexual orientation.

One of Lebanon's LGBTQ rights group, HELEM, called for the protests with the slogan, '**Stand up against the tests of shame, vaginal or anal.**'... HELEM also voiced solidarity with arrested women who were subjected to 'virginity tests' showing the invasive procedure as a gender-based crime, rather than a queer one.

Police men preforming illegal anal tests on queer people in underground dens... not to *queer* the perception of the reader, but this situation appears to fall into the fetishized and queer systematic practices of Arab culture.

Surely, the *queer* and *sadistic* nature of the act of *anal policing* should remind the reader of the jailed afghan women, who were often subjected to forced and degrading virginity tests. Most of the times, even when their tests came out negative, the doctor just wrote: "*The hymen is not broken, but it is possible that it was anal penetration*". His (of course!) statement sends people to jail and keeps bringing them back for more tests. The victim gets victimized again and again."[viii]

viii https://www.nytimes.com/2016/03/02/world/asia/jailed-afghan-women-are-often-subjected-to-virginity-tests-report-says.html

The rhetoric behind administering these tests is to de-subjectify the individuals for committing immoral acts.

In the Arab world, you only deserve to be a *subject* if you are a moral Arab object: A praying, prying and preying object of Arab heteronormativity: a beacon of Arabness and a guardian for God-given Arab virtues like virginity and chastity.

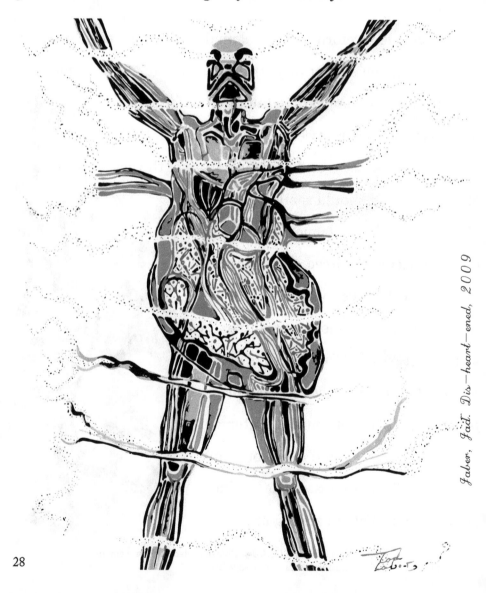

Faber, Jad. Dis-heart-ened, 2009

Fall morally short, and you are no longer an object deserving of subjectivity and that is grounds for all kinds of systematic, judicial and cultural abuses that range from shoving a boiled egg down someone's anus[ix] as proof of their queerness, to, in the case of Arab women, traditional divorce.

You become subservient, subconsciously...

The test of shame is a *daily* ritual for Arab queers, who are "tested" on their ability to seamlessly camouflage into the queer-hating, queer-fetishizing environment of Arab culture. The test does not have to happen in underground jail cells by police members, it can happen in broad daylight, in a warm home, over a morning cup of coffee by the queer's aunt or mother.

We are the culture that maneuvers around *shame*,

To *contain*, and *refrain*, and *restrain*,

So shame is not "tagged" upon our family *name*.

What is shame's function in society? It negotiates tirelessly with the autonomy of the person, controlling at first their behavior, then their thought.

---

ix   What is known as the "Anal test of shame" for Queer Arabs, to verify if they are "bottoms" or "receivers", more so than if they are queer.

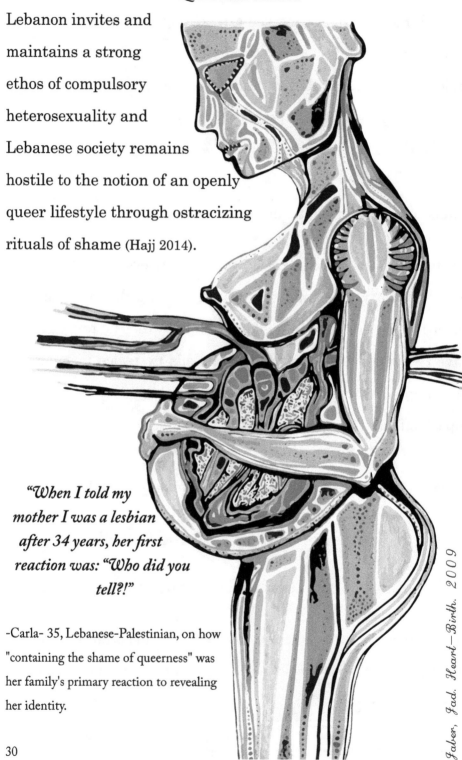

Lebanon invites and maintains a strong ethos of compulsory heterosexuality and Lebanese society remains hostile to the notion of an openly queer lifestyle through ostracizing rituals of shame (Hajj 2014).

"When I told my mother I was a lesbian after 34 years, her first reaction was: "Who did you tell?!"

-Carla- 35, Lebanese-Palestinian, on how "containing the shame of queerness" was her family's primary reaction to revealing her identity.

Jaber, Fadi. Heart-Birth. 2009

Shame is a *more* powerful weapon in collective cultures, and Arabs do *shameful* things to *avoid* it.

It becomes the moral rhetoric itself, even if it entails behaving immorally.

This book pays respect to all those Arab women that have undergone female circumcision, the young girls lost to honor crimes, and the queer boys who have committed suicide in loneliness and despair.

They, amongst many others, are victims of Arab shame.

> *"I gained weight at eighteen, which prompted my widowed father to make comments about how disproportional my body was. He wanted me to get married early and leave the house. Become another man's responsibility. Having a belly and a small chest, he said, made my chances slim."*
>
> -Alia, 33, Lebanon, on getting her breast implants at 19.

Alia also mentioned that her father forcibly sent her to the United States for the procedure to avoid the shame of the family knowing. He insisted she gets her implants *under* the breast muscle, an extremely painful procedure at the time, so that "she can quickly marry and still be able to breast feed" (her father's words).

31

THE

LIBIDINAL

QUEER SHAKRA

Jaber, Jad. The Ghosted Tree, 2011

CHAPTER FOUR

The Libidinal Queer Shakra

Is sexuality *more* important than existence?

"The sexual mayhem that is Lebanon has more than shaped my existence. It has shaped my sexuality."

- Mostafa, 37, Beirut

Many like Plato, Socrates, Freud and Lacan amongst others, have subversively and literally stated that sexuality *is* existence.

"My mother asked me, "Is it worth loosing everything that you are, just for being queer?"

- Haytham, 29, Jordan

In the space of a few centuries, a certain inclination has led us to direct the question of *what* we are, *to* sex. Not so much to sex *as* representing nature, but to sex as *history*, as *signification* and *discourse*. We have placed ourselves under the sign of sex (Foucaulat 1990, 78).

THERE IS NOTHING PERIPHERAL ABOUT HUMAN SEXUALITY...

Even if non-existent or eradicated, as it *seems* to be in the public spaces of the Arab world, its *non-existence* is an indication of Arab culture's ability to fetishize what it sanctions. Identifiable queer behavior is heavily sanctioned in the Arab world. Queer in that sense is everything that falls outside the ordinances of heteronormative culture.

Queer is gender neutral.

Queer is home to the shamed.

"I was ostracized after my divorce. Men looked at me like prey, and women looked at me like a predator out to get their husbands. There was no place for me at wedding tables, within family invite cards, for morning gatherings with the ladies."

– Asma, 42, Syria

Veiling beautiful, long, lush hair neither eradicates the existence of the hair or the hair's power to fetishize and *be* fetishized by the male gaze.

If anything, is hair, like queer, even *more* pleasurable when unveiled?

Could Arabs be addicted to fetishizing the process of unveiling itself, regardless of the object or subject underneath?

"I was new in the Gulf and was invited by my friend to a party. The house had a private section, with a central room and private bedrooms around the center. They pointed me to the party's owner, a prince. He did not address any of the men in the room. He just had his eye on our drinks, which he ordered his Indian workers to fill up incessantly. The women then came. All in Burqas. They went directly into the bedrooms and came out almost naked. They were Moroccan, Syrian, Saudi, Iraqi, Egyptian. The party had a lot of Hashish and cocaine. Suddenly, the lights went out. The music stopped. Worried, I turned to my friend asking him if something was wrong. "Just the call for prayer" he said. "The party resumes after the prayer stops…give it a few minutes"

-Talal , 41, Lebanese

Why do all these cultural convolutions and layers exist? Why is all this time invested in sanctions, formalities and collective illusions? How can *all* these queer Arab subjects exist when Arab culture consistently states that they do not?

"We have no queers here. Why would we, my son? We all come from close nuclear households. God would not inflict us with this disease."

-Haidar, 48, South of Lebanon

Even if skewed, *perverted*, *domiciled*, *oppressed*, or *repressed*...

Even *if* banned on the streets, *before* marriage, *after* divorce, in public spaces and in schools... The Arab *sexual* shakra is *still*[x] omnipresent in *all* of the queer's subjectivity and *most* Arab spaces and identities.

It is a sexual energy that affects *all* aspects of human existence, including one's perception, decision-making and consciousness. It cannot be de-subjectified or confined.

x   The queer Arab collective *still* exists against all odds, such as public and private institutional discrimination, religious discrimination, and familial discrimination and ostracism...

The queer shakra *in* Arabs is a *deeply* rooted tree of energy. As "trees teach us about life", the *stronger* the winds *push* against them, the *deeper* their roots dig.

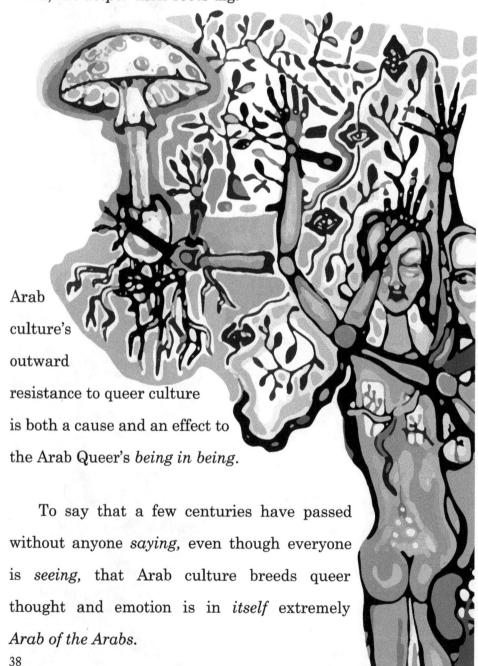

Arab culture's outward resistance to queer culture is both a cause and an effect to the Arab Queer's *being in being*.

To say that a few centuries have passed without anyone *saying*, even though everyone is *seeing*, that Arab culture breeds queer thought and emotion is in *itself* extremely *Arab of the Arabs*.

Through its anti-queer, hyper-masculine, hyper-religious, hyper-conformist rhetoric, Arabs develop antidotal queerness. The poison of pious Arab heteronormativity is dilapidated and stifling for *even* Arabs to handle. Queerness creates a habitable environment for heteronormativity to culturally persist.

"I find closeness in Khaliji men undeniable. They butterfly kiss with their noses, almost touching lips, everytime they say hello. They touch and hold hands as part of their expression of masculinity"

- Ghassan, 31, Syrian-Lebanese

We are the culture of the public secret.

That conceptual line of dissonance between public and private and that obvious oxymoron is what strong queer free subjects can eradicate, and Arabs have a fear of eradicating this specific cultural mantle. It is where all the status quos are rooted, where family hierarchies and gender norms are reinforced.

What would happen if all these chains and ties came undone? Arabs would be free.

The social masquerade existent is thus premised on a power asymmetry, an example of which would be the subordination of queer visibility to the hetero-normative requirements of the status quo (Hajj 2014).

The *sexualized* nature of the queer Arab martyr goes further to prove the *necessity* of perceiving the sexual dimension of individual behavior and Arab culture from both an "Emic" *and* "Etic"[xi] (Michael W. Morris 1999) lens.

Can an Arab queer author like myself divulge the secrets of the queer harem and the queer subject, without disrupting the *pleasure* that comes with *keeping* it a secret.

The Phenomenon [xii](Kant 1998) of queer martyrdom might *feel*, and *feeling* is the purpose of writing this book, like it *exclusively* targets the Arab LGBTQ community, but the "queer" in this book is *pansexual*[xiii].

Faber, Fad. The Third-Person Queer, 2004

xi   "Emic" and "Etic" refer to two kinds of field research done and viewpoints obtained: emic, from *within* the social group (from the perspective of the subject) and etic, from *outside* (from the perspective of the observer)

xii   "Phenomenon" (Kant)- the thing as it appears to an observer as *opposed* to "Noumenon"- the thing-in-itself.

xiii   The word Pansexual is reflective of those who feel they are sexually/emotionally/spiritually capable of falling in love with all genders

"I never felt like limiting myself to one sexual orientation or gender identity… and my adult sexual experience reflected that. Queerness though, is something I always felt"

–Lama-Lebanese-Palestinian, 37

As queer, Arab, *and* pansexual, the libidinal language of this book takes a leap of faith, a *leap* into the absurd; a reckless abandonment of reason (Friedman 1986) into the philosophical understanding of a *first-person* subject of the "I/ Queer/ Arab", as *sexual* and *existential* truth (Sartre, 1957*)*.

It is forbidden to be a *first-person* queer Arab because it brings shame to the queer subject and its corresponding families. One is forcibly queer in *third-person* in the Arab world. Arab queers speak of *themselves* as third-person queer and rant their pro-queer/anti-queer opinions in third-person. Telling culture what culture has been telling *them* all this time: "It's not me! It's *them*!". The problem is, when no one identifies as first-person queer, that category of *"them"* is passed along until it is pushed into oblivion. That is when Arab culture becomes comfortable enough to state it is anti-queer and houses no queers in its homes.

Language feels like self-betrayal during moments like these.

The queer feels dissonance as it utters words that separate *it* from *it*self. It would be speaking to the deaf if it uttered *queer first-person* words. Queers are forced to speak in the *only* language heteronormative ears absorb: *heteronormative* language.

> *"Ok, you can speak about the subject (queerness) but do not tell them it is you. No one should know. Even if they appear to accept it (queerness), let me see their faces when you tell them one of their own children is queer."*
>
> – M.J, 24, recalling a conversation with his mother regarding publically discussing the topic of queerness in the Arab world.

The martyr is that who has the courage to be the first-person subject of the "I/ Queer/ Arab".

The martyr is the unveiled, unfiltered, and holistic Arab queer "noumenon"[xiv] (I. a. Kant 1998).

The martyr chooses to be placed as a queer subject in Arab history for the greater cause of *the truth* through writing, creating, and representing what is within. All my writings may be considered tasks imposed from within, their source was a fateful compulsion assailed from within myself. I permitted the spirit that moved me, to speak out (Jung, 1963).

---

xiv "Noumenon" -The thing in itself as *opposed* to "Phenomenon" the thing as it appears to the observer.

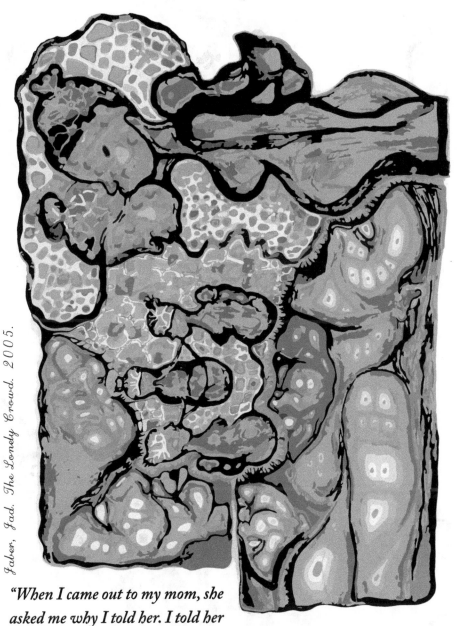

Faber, Fad. The Lonely Crowd. 2005.

"When I came out to my mom, she
asked me why I told her. I told her
because I needed to live in truth and voice my truth. She said she wished
she died without knowing; that theirs is not a generation of truth, but
of respecting values and traditions and other's feelings. "I never told you
about my sexual preferences, why should you?" she said."

-Jihad, 34, Lebanon

5

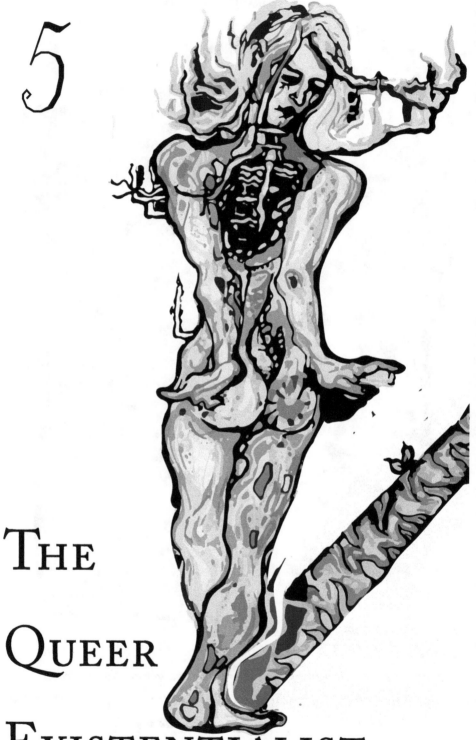

THE

QUEER

EXISTENTIALIST

Faber, Fad. The Cultivated Self, 2005

Queer Arab
Essence Versus Existence

The Queer Existentialist:
Queer Arab Essence Versus Existence

To support the queer's ability to cause change within itself[xv] and society, is to *suppose* an *existential* fate for the queer. A fate *not* bound by the essence *society* has imprinted on it: namely, the abnormal, the abomination and the abhorrent essence of Arab queerness.

> *"Don't pass your contagious mental sickness to our kids. Why you are you showing us this? It is against nature! Arabs are not like that!"*

-Local Arab Facebook user commenting on Queer rights videos by the Arab Foundation for Freedom and Equality.

The queer fate should also *not* be bound by the essence the queer has invested in *itself*. An essence it presumes as its *own* and *true* essence: a meek, dejected and negotiating essence.

---

xv   The Arab queer is often described in the book as an **"it"**, neither a *he*, or a *she*, nor an *"in-between"*, because all these identities have *"subjectivity"*, namely a name, place, image, representation, institutional and judicial and cultural rights, etc.... which the queer *lacks*. The book itself attempts to bring light to this *lack* of subjectivity.

The possibility that a *new* queer subjectivity *can* be born, as both Arab and queer, might alter the essence and the fate of the queer.

Can *queer* be reborn in arab culture as the new *normal*?

"I don't think I would ever come back. Not even in ten years. They can never accept us. Would my kids be able to play in the family garden as the other kids? The garden passed to me by ten generations of my family? Probably not. That garden belongs to normal Arab families"

-Danny, Lebanese, about moving back to Lebanon from Canada with his partner and adopted children.

The possibility of *that* birth hinges on *reintroducing* the concept of existentialism to Arab queers, to encourage them to live and dream *outside* the ordinances of heteronormative culture.

To not dare to dream outside Arab thoughts is the ultimate queer oppression.

If queers are fearful of putting queer emotions and images in their subconsciousness, the possibility of dreaming about being a whole queer subject becomes dim: how many girls have dreamt about being rescued by a prince on a white horse? Many.

Ever wondered why?

Dreams are non-linear, but the soul still s(peaks) loudly through them: it speaks through images and metaphors. Not having positive metaphors for same-sex love and queer subjects increases the queer's fear of absorbing queerness because we fear most what we do not know. Queers become impermeable to dreaming queerly thereby resisting the possibility of positive change.

A central concept of which Sartre has based Existentialism on is that "existence precedes essence" (Sarte 1978, 36). To break that down practically, a subject or object's *existance* is more important than its *essence*. A couch, an object, might me created and essembled to be used as a sitting space, its *essence*. Your family members though, might be using it to sleep, its *existence*. The couch's essence was not necessarily paralleled by its existence.

To move this concept from a couch to humanity, the *essence* of religion might be to bring love, peace and forgiveness, but its *existence* has mostly brought religious wars and destruction

Man, according to Abrahamic theology was made to serve god, his *essence,* while man exists to serving himself, his *existence.* So a specific identity, such as the Arab queer, does not *need* to *exist* within the mold or design built for it by Arab culture, because it *is* *"its"* *choice,* to exist *outside* that purpose.

"We are the culture of Adarak wu Nasibak[xvi]: how can we make real change? How can we separate religion from the state? How can we be free?"

–Tamara, 29, Lebanon

"existence precedes essence"

What is Arab culture's purpose to depicting queers as abnormal? The purpose is to distinctly *define* the normal. The purpose is also to strike fear through the fate of the queer, the distinct "other", so that young boys and girls know exactly how to keep the heteronormative charades running.

With every negative queer representation, the "right of heteronormativity" is contrasted and reemphasized on the expense of the "wrong of queerness".

xvi   Arabic for Fate and Fated: in Arabic culture, the use of fate colloquially is extremely common. Individuals are seen as fated towards success, love, failure, or sickness.

The embodiment of the philosophy of existentialism describes the power of *existing, making* your own choices, *carving* your own fate, versus abiding or living *for* that intangible essence.

The queer might be forced to be "the other" to Arab culture, but it should not be "the other" to itself.

It should feel coalesced.

Faber, Jad. *The Coalesced Schizophrenic. 2006*

The real danger of suppressing queer thought is when the queer subject cannot reform and re-gather, to resist and exist.

SO WHY HAVE ARAB QUEERS *CHOSEN* NOT TO EXIST AS QUEER *AND* ARAB?
TO *EXIST* BY THE ESSENCE WHICH THEY *FEEL?*

It might be easy to pinpoint this *eternal* state of martyrdom, to the queer's "weak" sense of self. But we forget that Arab queers lack *agency*, best described as an individual's ability to make his or her own free choices and act independently and autonomously, *without* the control of specific social structures like religion, customs, ethnicity, class, and gender.

HOW CAN WE EXPECT A *STRONG* SENSE OF SELF, FROM A SUBJECT THAT LACKS *AGENCY?*

With *acquitting* Arab queers of some of their existential responsibility, the real *culprit,* Arab society, is moved to the forefront. Arabs *themselves* created the negative representation of the modern queer *it,* to *serve* the purpose of being "the other". *Their* "heteronormative" values are re-invigorated with every passing *visible* queer, with every *soft* voice, every *tampered* walk, and every *wrong-pointing* wrist. These Queer red flags cause cultural distraught!

Surprisingly, before these recent cultural developements, hetero-queerness was the norm for Arabs.

"Kuwaiti men love to forget their history! We know of the men who were men enough to dress as women like Ali Al-Rasheed! 50's Kuwaiti theatre shows our real impression of feminine men; we like them!"

-Ahmed, 40, Kuwait

Somewhere, an Arab mom points towards a queer subject with *her* children, and *warns* them about becoming "mkhanath"[xvii], and once again, young masses are "huffed and puffed into hetero-normalization" by the big, bad, *queer* wolf.

Mothers *more* often than fathers, attempt to reinstitute Arab heteronormative rules and values aggressively. Reasons might be fear for the fate of the children to exist outside culturally accepted ordinances.

Another reason is the gendered structure to Arab household management where women do the feminized labor.

xvii   Feminine/ Faggot

Women are *more* involved with their children and *more* "home-bound", thereby experiencing a level of *closeness* to their children that men rarely experience. Hence women bear the bigger responsibility of nurturing society's values into the children, with working father figures being more absent.

> *" Look mama, this hotel is where this gay man killed himself. Gays always kill or get killed. You have to be conscious of your urges, so you do not end up like that "*
>
> -Jihad, 31, recalling his mother's warning when he was 12.

Young queer martyrs socially survive through martyring their essence and learning that the *queer* "other" is anti-Arab, and more so, anti-human. Yet, they associate with *that* same "other" *within*.

Forced to martyr with either their consciousness, *or* their queer voice and representation, they martyr their consciousness when they deny the queer *within* and repudiate that colorful internal "difference". In contrast, they are forced to martyr their voice and representation, *if* they choose to develop their queer consciousness.

"If we have the courage, we can say it to ourselves, but not the world"

-Sara, Lebanon, 22

Even though Arabs have a history with being "queer friendly" and *non*-gender bound, they have covered up their collective queer Id[xviii], behind an Arab Super-ego, rooted and nurtured by patriarchy, piety, politics, and of-course that geopolitical struggle with the West.[xix] It seems now more than ever, with Arabs immigrating into queer-friendly and gender fluid environments, that The West has its own say towards the way Arabs run things: there exists a conscious level of Western involvement in Arab dirty laundry.

"White Europeans protesting in Denmark against the Burqa Ban in their country is equivalent to Arabs in Iraq protesting GMO use in Canada: Who the hell put you in the middle of this? A proof of blind activism. What are you cheering on? What are you advocating, do you know? Have you lived it? Have you been veiled by a Burqa before?"

-Abir, 31, reacting to Danish protests against the Burqa Ban.

xviii   The Id, ego, and super-ego are the three connected agents in Freud's model of the psyche. The Id contains the humans' instinctual drives.

xix   Pinkwashing, the phenomenon of describing specific products/ nationalities/ regimes as "Gay-Friendly", to be seen as tolerant, progressive, modern, and liberal. Arabs have the tendency to view Israel and the USA as gay-friendly, and queer culture tends to be viewed as belonging to that Pinkwashed Western discourse.

With the Internet at the queer fetal fingers, that subjectivity is *choosing* to change its "tagged" essence, and is venturing to *form* one of its own. The Arab queer represents the ultimate existential struggle for identity.

Going back to Sartes, questioning if the Arab queer's existence precedes his essence, does not answer the inherent question *within* the question, namely what is the *present* essence of the Arab Queer? It is what the Queer "is": The "Idea" of the queer, by the queer *and* by its hosting context, Arab society. It is the Queer's nature *and* content.

The image painted before us of the queer martyr's essence is unclear and tainted, and the reason it is as such, versus an image of an LGBT couple in New York, is because Arab queers lack representation. They also lack a history, but they should not. They just need to *comb out* all these same-sex, gender-fluid occurences and queer subjects from Arab history and mythology.

"I loved watching men cross-dressing in old black and white Egyptian movies. Even Om Kolthoum dressed as a Bedouin boy. No one would dare put this on TV anymore. The Muslim brotherhood and conservatives would go crazy. Even though the Internet opened some doors, there is less space for gays and lesbians to show themselves now"

-Zainab, 24, Egypt

6

THE PHENOMENAL
EVENT OF...

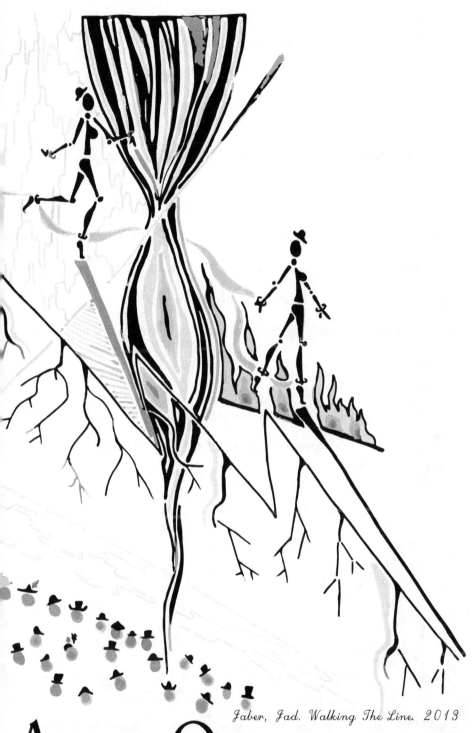

Jaber, Jad. Walking The Line. 2013

ARAB QUEERNESS

Chapter Six

The Phenomenal Event of Arab Queerness

The phenomenon of Queerness in the Arab world is a debatable, even violent subject that differs in content depending on two different perspectives: one of which is the West's perspective[xx] of queerness in the Arab world, and the other is the Arab world's perspective[xxi] of its own queer culture..

Let us look at an example of how the phenomenon of queerness compromises the queer numina, and intentions.

An Arab, self-identifying as queer, wants to experience queerness.

Experience in general is broken down into *intentionality* towards a specific *goal*.

xx   The discourse perceived as the "Gaze of the West", namely of Europe and the USA, towards LGBT culture in the Arab World, depicted in visual media, movies and news stations such as CNN, BBC, and social media, such as Facebook.
xxi   The discourse towards Queer Arab culture, depicted by Arab visual media and social media, such as the Lebanese Broadcasting Corporation International, and other local and national news stations like Al-Jazeera.

This consciously directed intentionality is related to the perceived nature of the object. *For example, being charitable is related to the "intrinsic good" perceived in charitable acts.* That is why people do charity, and why philanthropy is perceived as a virtue. In terms of the Arab queer, there is a *lacking* intentionality when pursuing the object of Arab queerness.

To draw a comparison to the example of charity, being (or not being) queer is related to the "intrinsic good" (or bad) perceived in queer acts.

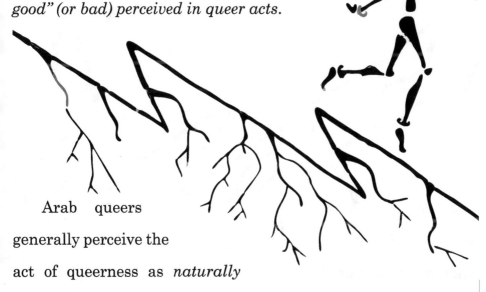

Arab queers generally perceive the act of queerness as *naturally* and *deeply* wrong. Moreover, not behaving queerly *or* identifying as queer is a *requirement* of public survival and most of the time, identity-survival.

As *people* can see the natural *good* in charity, *Arabs* have been nurtured to see the natural *bad* in queerness.

They lost attention to *how* their intentions towards their queerness have changed after years of shadowed negotiations. They then *reduced* their queer subjectivity to "that event", that behavior, that language, and that *imagined* essence.

"It was the first time I had done it; it hurt badly and he didn't use protection. Nothing like this had ever happened in our family or to my friends. He finished and left. Did not say a word. When I grew older, I was able to see how that event had influenced my first relationships"

-Majed, 27, Syria

Even if queerness *is* an "event" in the Arab world, its sporadic, repetitive, *event-ness* constitutes a reality *worth* anatomizing: a truth of the queer martyr's *state*. Connecting these events, as realizations of truth, creates the holistic image of the Arab queer subjectivity. The event is in no way a void, or a stupor, separated from what *becomes*...it is the concentration of the continuity of life and its intensification (badiou 2007).

The continuous, undeniable, events of queerness in both Arab culture and the queer subject bring us to an ontological truth about the power that brought queerness to a culture that systematically resists it; the power that *birthed* it; namely, Arab culture. Queer essence was not born of a void, but was born of the queer *essence essentially* existing in Arab culture.

To say that queers share the *same* essence with Arab culture, which has cultivated their existence, is to depict a modern geopolitical and cultural state of existence for queers, where they are *both* wanted and rejected, *both* fetishized and castrated. This modern state for the Arab queer has been seen before in Western queer history and American mainstream politics that changed dramatically in the 1980's as discourses of morality and sexual repression came to dominate a public sphere that was *both* newly hospitable and newly hostile to LGBTQ people (Potter, 2006).

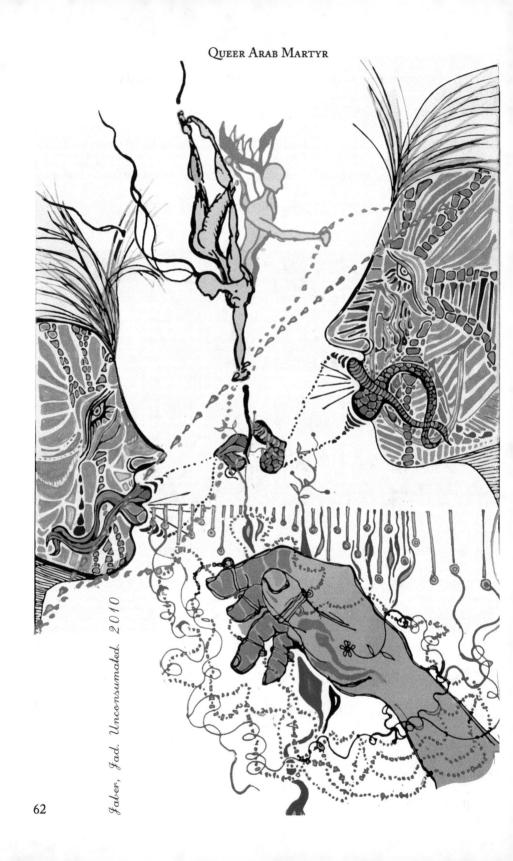

Faber, Fadi. Unconsumated. 2010

Could we *now* be in a period of queer Arab evolution that is heading in a similar direction to the West?

"In my culture, rarely do you come out. But when you do, it is really them that come out to you: their truth and feelings towards the subject. It takes you to come out, so that their truth comes out: and most come out as bigots. Very few remain friends and family"

-Charbel, Lebanon, 24, on coming out in the Arab world

Whether that "event of positive change" will happen in the Arab world, depends on the queer subject's power of bringing *attention to its real essence* for both itself and Arab culture, one "coming-out story" at a time.

"Every queer Arab that comes out to their parents is doing their own small revolution. The other option is lying and hiding.
When I came out to my parents, I knew that they could no longer look and talk about gays the way they used to with their friends, because now, their own son is gay. That is social change."

-Omar, 29, Jordanian

63

7

Jaber, Jad. The Shattered Ego, 1998

THE QUEER
ATTENTION TO ITS
INTENTION

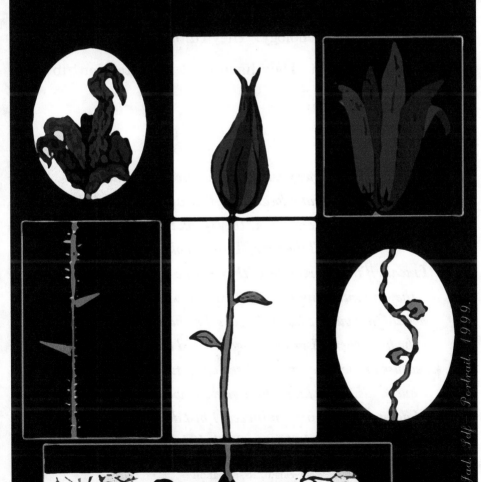

Faber. Jad. Self — Portrait. 1999.

Chapter Seven

The Queer Attention to Its Intention

How can queers exist as publically heteronormative, and *not* have that existential and behavioral "compromise" seep into their consciousness and psychology? They *cannot*. They have already *martyred* their content. They have paid no "attention" to their "intentions" (Grosz 1986).

"Sometimes my gay friends address me as a woman and not any woman, but a local, over-feminine, over-polished, typical Lebanese woman. They speak this way to each other all the time, "Laiki ya okhti^{xxii}".
I mean, if they conversed with the same Lebanese women they are imitating in order to speak to each other, they would find out she hates the gays. She hates them because she finds them disgusting, against god and family, and because for her, they are a missed opportunity at becoming husbands. If her kids where gay, she would kill herself. I do not mind being feminized. I just do not want to be addressed like that homophobic Lebanese woman."

-Shadi, 26, Lebanon

xxii   "Hey Sister" in colloquial Lebanese.

At the level of the symbol, society is the main stakeholder, nurturing via laws and education, via its all-seeing eye, ideas of conventional behavior, moral stances, and definitions of perfection, of nature. *All* of which might be *reshuffling* the queer's natural instinct, its innate trajectory, homeostasis, and its self-preserving intentions. Therefore, Instinct is anything but a blind and indefinite impulse, since it proves to be attuned and adapted to a definite external situation (Carl Jung; The Undiscovered Self; Page 49). In Laccanian term, being part of the social world entails the individual's separation from their natural bodily drives, "jouissance", and their movement away from nature, into culture (Lacan, 1968).

In terms of the Arab queer, the space between *their* nature and their culture is already an abyss. It is already *too* far to merge, for according to culture, the queer nature *does not* and *cannot* exist in Arab sovereign space, thought and spirit.

"Just kill them"

-Alaa, 31, Lebanese, university professor recalling his students' reactions

in class to the possibility of them having queer children.

Looking at Lacan's notion of the "loss of jouissance to culture", *relinquishing one's nature for culture* is *how* the queer Arab severed from its nature and became an "It".

Hence, The Arab Queer is no longer a he or she. *It* is an "It".

It is the Monster to its Monstrosity!

"I mean he was the one staring at me in the locker room. That is how you know someone is interested here since they can never tell you. During the shower, I knocked on his shower door to ask for shampoo, and he just opened and punched my face in. I felt hurt and embarrassed. He told all management I was trying to touch him."

-Wissam, 18, Lebanon

The queer is not "allowed" to be aware of the true *nature* of the object and "event" of queerness in Arab society because it is short-lived and layered with the appearances of hetero-normativity. For most of the time, what the Arab queer *perceives* to be the right and natural way of existing *as* queer, is a regurgitation of society's manual.

The queer is *intentionally* pursuing an object of an entirely different nature to its own, *unintentionally* defying its intentions, which begs the question...

How *individual* is "Arab Intentionality" to begin with?

To answer that question, Arab queers *unintentionally* behave with themselves, the way Arab society behaves with them. Arab queers have contained and deformed the object of queerness, as Arab society has taught them to do.

"Why are you interested in her? (Pointing at a male dancer on the podium) She is effeminate and looks like she has AIDS"

– Hussein, self-proclaimed queer, 23, Beirut

Arab intentionality might be a false "event" in itself, in a culture *so* collective, that public thought has *already* compromised private thinking. A scenario of a collective brainwash, institutionalized and grounded in gendered spaces and images that become the fertile grounds for queerness to *grow*. Queerness also seems to grow *within* the archetype of the hyper-masculine, prideful, and religious Arab.

Some might even pinpoint *that* queer growth as the growth of the real, individual, and organic subject, in an Arab object[xxiii].

xxiii   A moral Arab object: A praying, prying and preying object of Arab heteronormativity.

Arab society births and indoctrinates Arab objects by the millions, yet it cannot indoctrinate that which it has not made visible or created a language for. Like a Chinese bamboo tree that lays dormant for four years, only to grow eighty feet tall in just six weeks once it reaches its fifth year, queerness is nurtured and grows under Arab grounds: the more it lays dormant, the more it yearns to explode out and show its stature. The question is of course, *what it is growing into*, considering that its *own* mother, society, has outwardly and consistently aborted the Arab queer fetus for decades.

> *"In Kuwait, government/public schools are fully segregated, while private schools had girls. People were comfortable identifying as gay in government schools from a very early age and having queer sex while in middle school. They felt so accepted at school that they would be fine identifying as gay by the time they reach adulthood. My friends in private school on the other hand, were all uncomfortable and closeted about being gay, up until they reached college."*

-Walid, 28, Kuwaiti

Aborted and resurrected *over* history, Arab queers are martyrs that keep being reborn into existence and the *essence* from which they are born from is Arab through-and-through. To say that Arab culture is not *essentially* queer is *false*. Radical Arabic heteronormalists can be *shown* how their anti-queer discourse has become the *womb* from which beautiful Arab queerness is born.

In terms of martyring the queer's intentionality or "intuition", the queer cannot know the nature of the possibility of freedom, being that the appearances of all that he has absorbed and learned is radically opposing to queer existence. In the appearances and violence, it attempts to find truth.

> *"I felt like a queer child and I couldn't be. So I just never felt like a child. Instead, I always felt like an adult in a child's body. At the age of twelve, I would ritually masturbate with my friend to straight porn, and we would ejaculate separately in the toilet. One time, I found his sperm still stuck on the sink. I recall feeling taken over and not myself, and I touched it. I recall looking back at myself in the mirror in shame, and wondering if that mirror had eyes"*

-Rami, 34, Saudi Arabia

The possibilities the Arab queer *wishes for* in terms of *freedom* are not *free* at all. They are part of *that* world of appearances. All our intuition is nothing but the representation of appearance. The things which we intuit are not in themselves what we intuit them as being, nor their relations so constituted in themselves as they appear to us (Kant 1781).

Arab queers are victim to this false intuition, as they are their own prisoners in terms of presuming that this intuition is universal and *natural*. This presumption comes from the "ethical war" raised against them, causing them to replace *their* queer subjectivity with the *collective* subjectivity.

71

That is their coping mechanism to face the ongoing "ethical violence", best described as ethical injunctions that terrorizes them with their brutal imposition of their universality (S. Zizek, The Structure of Domination Today: A Lacanian View 2004).

Arab *queers* have martyred their intentions, and with that, the attention to their culturally imposed intentions is *also* subdued.

"Seriously, gay equality? I mean, I am gay, but to put it like this in the face of Arab culture is just so rude. Out gays and gays that want equality and marriage are really pushing it too far. How far do they want to go? Ayb! [xxiv]*"*

- Philip, Self-

proclaimed queer,

Lebanon, 31

xxiv Ayb: Colloquial Lebanese for "Shame on them".

72

Are *Arab queers* **aware** that their heteronormative disguises and masks are *not* their actual bodies and faces?

Are *Arab queers* **aware** that their puns and insults towards one another actuate and perpetuate the *same* language as the society they are *resisting*?

Are *Arab queers* **aware** that their representation recreates the *same* gendered binaries and hierarchies that have *held* them in place as the "untouchables" of Arab-Islamic society?

Are *Arab queers* **aware** of the sweeping meaning of revolution, or do they negotiate *down* their revolutions with society and family, to bashful, isolated, infrequent, convoluted acts of resistance?

Faber, Jad. The Loving Martyr, 2006

THE QUEER ARAB TONGUE

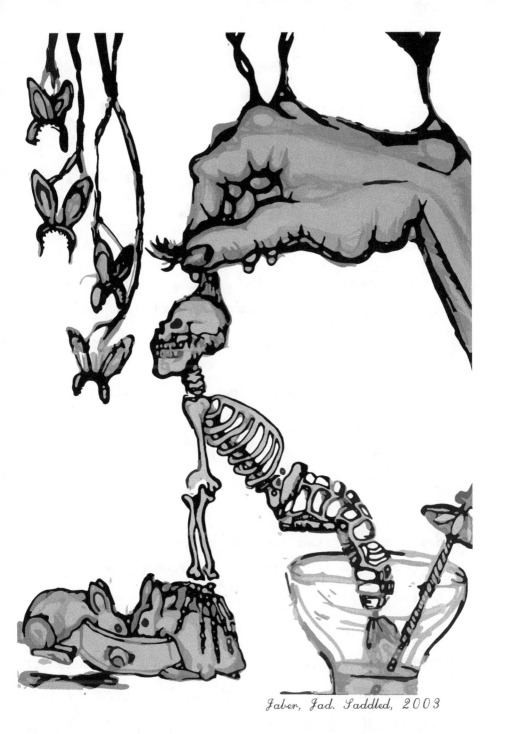

Jaber, Jad. Saddled, 2003

And Self Prohibition

CHAPTER EIGHT

The Queer Arab Tongue and Self Prohibition

"I knew that gay sex was prohibited, but I also did not masturbate while feeling gay" - "Why? I did not know it was allowed"

-Fouad, Kuwait, 32

Sometimes, societies force their prohibitions. They implement them through family, friends, and even social institutions around the queer, such as the law, religion, work, and school. At other times, the queer forces prohibitions upon *him* or *herself*.

"A friend of mine, who was outwardly feminine in behavior and "queer" in appearance, was once refused bread. Yes, bread from a bakery."

-Lucas, 34

To put that in a practical context, the Arab queer *disallows* him or herself from engaging in the "real normal" because "society's normal" has no space for their identity. The queer eventually prohibits it-self from acts of self-preservation, self-release, self-expression, and of course, self-acceptance.

A Heteronormative subject does not *need* permission and clearance to masturbate to his or her fantasies and fetishes.

> *"She caught me playing with the Barbie.*
> *The shame I felt, the feeling of being*
> *exposed, caught off-guard in my act of*
> *queerness, stayed with me from then until*
> *my late twenties"*

-Haidar, 29, 2018, recalling an incident with his mother when he was 11.

When does society's prohibition of "queer performativity" *become* the self- prohibition of the queer subject? When the jurisdictions of queer thought, language and subjectivity in society translate to the queer's internal processes.

When society refuses to *pronounce* queerness, the queer has the task of uttering it for him or herself for that first time, using a language that is cleansed of queer expression. Performing queerness for the first time also has a daunting effect, when the act is associated with being punished and has no visual or cultural predecessors, like neighbors who are a gay couple, or a lesbian-friendly TV show, or a queer sensitive sex Ed classes at School etc.

Performativity, like the act of marriage, embedded in a social network and its speech acts, brings and materializes the act of hetero-normalization.

"I pronounce you" puts into effect the relation that it names (Butler, 1993, 17), so keeping a subjectivity and its consequential language un-namable and unpronounceable, puts the relation the queer has to him or herself, in a state of remission and eventual *annihilation*.

Performative acts are forms of authoritative speech: statements, which, in their uttering, also perform a certain action and exercise a binding power on the action performed and the subjects performing them. The power of discourse to produce that which it names is thus essentially linked with the question of performativity (Butler, 1993, 17). The heteronormative Arab discourse, bound in a network of authorization and punishment, sanctions the performance of queerness through legal sentences, rituals, and religious courts and sermons. Hence, heteronormative Arab discourse cements its authoritative power by sanctioning and punishing the performativity of queerness and not having an appropriate cultural name for it.

Queer *thoughts* and *dreams* are the biggest threat to Arab authority. Queerness, as the Arabs fear, can trickle down and unscrew the shackles that have held women to their abusive husbands, obliged women to leave their careers to be good mothers, stopped young men from kissing their partners goodbye on the street, made cooking and sewing the ultimate skill for Arab girls, and sanctioned little boys from playing with Barbies.

Arab culture invests a lot of time in keeping the strings that tie it all together *tight*, and in fighting off foreign threats. If the threats are local, Arab culture will just starve them of positive cultural material, like a holistic language. Starve them until they perish from inanition.

It is from *that* imagined subjectivity and *that* queer dream that Arab queers can draw power to form a *full* subjectivity. The distinction between the prisoner who dreams of walking *just* outside the prison doors, and the prisoner who dreams of *running* in large open fields exemplifies *the power of the dream*. That is why dreaming and imagining freely is *that* thin portal where queer essence *can* pass into queer existence.

The question is what to do with the cultural vacuum following **THE DREAM?** The answer is, create, produce, put your name in history, but most importantly as your truth!

9

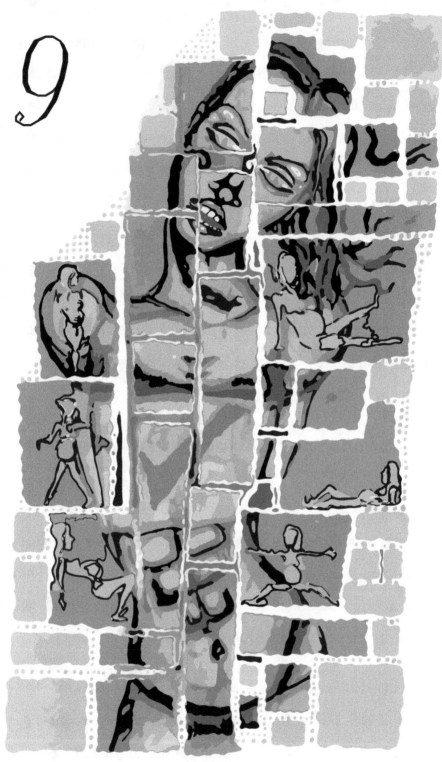

Jaber, Jad. Pregnant Fragments, 2004

I Queer, *Therefore I am*

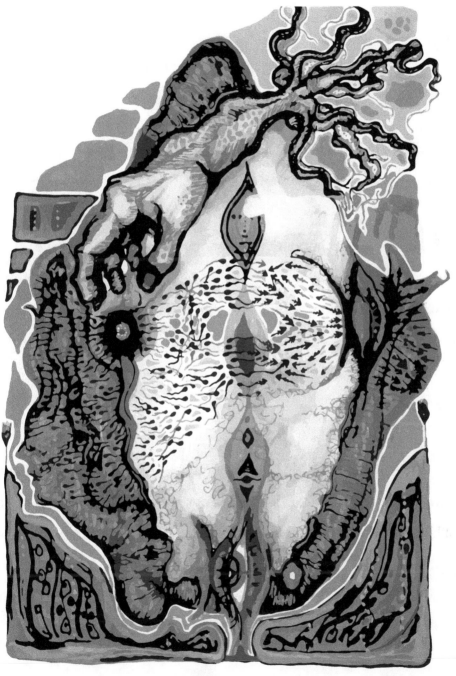

Faber, Jad. The Female Self. 2005

I Queer, Therefore I am

Where does the queer Arab martyr "cite" his or her queerness *from*, and *who* decides what can and cannot be "cited"?

The Arab archetypal judge is male, pious, collective, and heteronormative. What *that* judge is able to do is authorize and install the situation he names by invariably citing the law that he applies, and giving power to that citation. If he does not give power to that performance, the performance has no binding or conferring power.

According to Judith Butler, though it might appear that the *binding power* of the Arab judge is derived form the *natural* force of his will or from a prior authority and convention that is religious and patriarchal in nature, the *opposite* is true: that *binding power* is to be found *neither* in the subject of the judge *nor* in his will, but in the *citational legacy*.

It is often heard in Arab culture, that only *the man* can head a house, the man that should be represented in public, and the man that should be in the position of power, as Arab women have to *remain* privatized, feminine, chaste, and proper; these are all examples of *citational legacies*. This binding power of "*who* individuals are supposed to be and *how* they are supposed to behave" also controls women, queers, and their corresponding bodies and sexual histories. Empowered women, or women who act outside the bounds of hetero-normativity in the Arab world are not called bitches, they are called whores.

As women and queers find themselves being the minority of Arab culture, fighting for their rights entails knowing the void in the heteronormative judge's citation and knowing that his *binding power* has *no* power!

It is only though culture's constant act of citing it that it becomes an "already established will and authority" that is then used by the judge himself, to *naturalize* his power; it is that power which allowed a Muslim clerk to proclaim in god's name that Muslim women should not be purchasing or handling phallic shaped fruits and vegetables. That power is even more rooted in the conventional women themselves who *believed* and *felt* and warned their daughters, that purchasing a banana made them "whores".

That is the monstrosity of the binding power of authority; it makes the vulnerable subjects, like queers and women, the guards to their own prison. It is through the invocation of convention that the speech act of the judge derives its binding power and by which a contemporary (queer) act emerges in the context of a chain of binding conventions (Butler, 1993, 17).

Linguistically, Arab culture cites "Western language and thought" to describe queer performativity. Namely, the geopolitical western LGBTQ discourse, which does not always *apply* on queer Arab culture, yet this discourse, gives queer performativity a misplaced conferring power. Terms like "coming out" and "gay" are used in colloquial and formal language, between Arab queers and hetero-normatives alike, because there are no Arabic terms that describe these "events".

"I identified first with the language of religion, my friends and family, which felt shameful, blasphemous, and negative. "Gay" felt Ayb[xxv]. When I felt strong enough to abandon this local language, I fell into the colonialist wave of queerness and I defined my queerness through the White Western male; the one who has the most rights out of us and the one who is most visible. That identity was the first identity I could download. When I could no longer identify with the (aforementioned) rainbow flag subject, I started to identify more with a queer person of color; a queer minority" -Faysal, 27, Lebanese/ Syrian

xxv   Shameful/ Prohibited

Other than the queer language of the West, Arab culture also cites biologically deterministic and religious language and thought to describe queer performativity. An example of that would be "marid", which translates to ill, a biological term, and "Louti", a religious term which etymologically comes from The People of Lot; both are synonymous with queer.

The people of Lot, mentioned in the Quran, were the residents of the cities Gomorrah and Sodom, the ancient Islamic version of Gotham City, named after the Prophet Lot. The people ignored God's message of morality, monotheism, monogamy, and heterosexuality, so God destroyed the cities' sinful queer inhabitant. The word *Louti*, a colloquial Arab term, translates into "faggot".

Queers are represented in the Arab world as those that deserve penalty and extermination. Modern Muslim theorists would say that this is God's *divine will* towards the queers. Queer theorists would say that the people of Lot's sexual preferences were not the reason God destroyed it but other immoral acts, like stealing, cheating, lying, and killing. Therefore, the link between that destruction and homosexuality is a modern interpretation.

The history of "Profit Lot" linked to "Sodom", also associated queer culture to "Sodomy", further describing the queer subjectivity as a stigmatized sexual act or event, versus a holistic identity. 85

Arab culture's stance towards queerness is an indication of their instinct to sodomize as the sodomized gain pleasure in sodomizing others. In this scenario, sodomizing queerness has been fetishized by Arab culture.

Where can the queer cite his or her "I", when language does not serve the purpose of its full subject-formation? Some might say *"Shouldn't the identity and subjectivity of the queer, come before the development of his or her language?"* The reply to that would be where there is an "I" who utters or speaks and thereby produces an effect in discourse, there is first a discourse which precedes and enables that "I" and forms in language the constraining trajectory of its will. The queers Arab "I" cannot stands *behind* the discourse created by Arab culture and language. It cannot control or direct it, because it is *through* discourse, *through* being identified, named, and communicated back and forth, that the "I" comes to being. According to Butler (1993), this takes place prior to the "I"; it is the transitive invocation of the "I." If the "I" has no name in Arab culture, or only an English or French name, then it cannot come to being in an Arabic context.

As unnamable as queerness is to Arab society, it becomes unnamable to the Arab self. In Arab culture, the *other* common *"unnamable name"* is cancer, usually called locally "al-marad", *the* sickness.

One would *not* say, "he or she has cancer", but would say they got *the sickness* in Arabic with everyone *knowing* that "the sickness" is cancer. This "sickness" is not colloquially used on any other medical sicknesses, *except* cancer. Sadly enough, this name is also afflicted upon queer Arab people *when* self-identifying or identified as queer by Arab culture.

There are no "shades" of behavioral health in Arab culture. You are either healthy, or cancer(ous). And if you are "sick in your sexuality", your sexual cancer shall also be *unnamable.* Your queerness shall be *unnamable.* Indeed, I can only say "'I" to the extent that I have first been addressed, and that address has mobilized my place in speech. Paradoxically, social recognition *precedes and conditions* the formation of the subject. Recognition is not granted to a subject, but *forms* that subject.

The impossibility of a full recognition, that is, of ever fully inhabiting the name by which one's social identity is inaugurated and mobilized, implies the instability and incompleteness of subject-formation (Butler, 1993, 17). Hence, the Arab queer lacks the tools, one of which is the developed, subject-respecting language, to create a coalesced subjectivity: as it currently exists, it is an instable and incomplete subject.

"You know it's not true what they say, that we hate queers. Old Egyptian movies had so many cross-dressers, and many celebrities and even spiritual figures where gender fluid. But now, there is a fear of it, and people do not talk about it."

-Shadia, Egypt, 26

The queer has created its language, from society's puns and insults. It knows and thinks its queerness exists, but cannot find the space or words for it.

The queer, Arab, martyr attempts to bring the symptoms of having an incomplete subject formation into light, but more importantly, looks at the root causes of the void of its (mis) formation, one of which is its muted language and denied queer history.

It is *vital* that an Arab Queer can look *straight* into Arab Society's eyes, and say:

"I am the product of your culture"

"I am Arab and Queer"

"My essence is not to self-destruct after serving
the purpose of being
"the other""

"My essence is holistic
and well-rounded, and can
encompass being Arab, spiritual, familial,
successful, functional, as well as being queer"

"My essence has a past, present and future"

10

Faber, Fad. Queer Cadavers. 2011

THE QUEER PUBLIC SECRET

PLEASURE BEHIND THE BLIND EYE

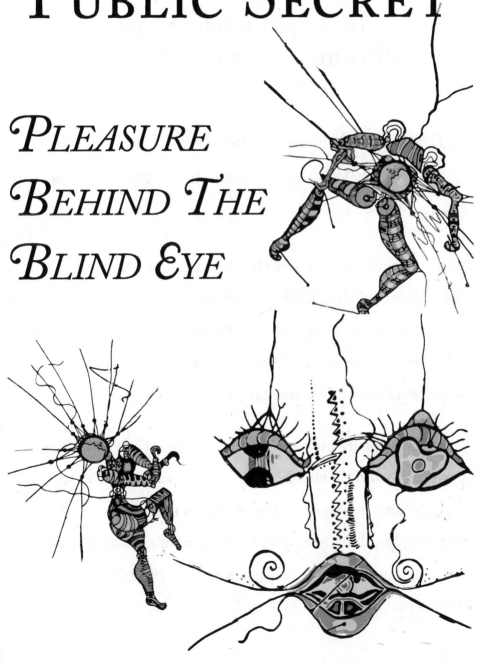

The Queer Public Secret: Pleasure Behind the Blind Eye

The notion of pleasure is fundamental to queer theory in the Arab world: **What occurs behind the "Blind Eye" in Arab culture?**

The Arab world is replete with these small pleasure hubs, where pleasure is exploded, after being held in its crest for millennia. Sometimes allowed legally, sometimes closed down, the *period* before their depletion is always the *phase* of the "Public Secret", the phase of the *highest* intensity.

These pleasure hubs are characterized by their own language, known as "word of mouth" or "Chinese whispers", as the *only* language and reference to the event, to that particular harem's *temporary* location: there is no building number, namable address or street sign: the event and place are not recorded in sounds or pictures and not even in history for that matter.

This fleeting, "already dead" *language* of the queer event is symbolic of the fleeting "already dead" *state* of queer existence within the Arab body. The Arab queer is *also* unable to name the *event of queerness* in its subjectivity. It can be called a "mistake in a car", a "phase in school", an "experiment in the alley", but neither the *object/ space* of queerness, nor the *subjects* of queerness, are represented or named.

It *is* sad that Arab history cannot encompass and register little queer love stories, but is it not even *sadder* that the Arab queer individual mind *also* expunges them to oblivion?

The harem is almost always on an empty beach, a bankrupted cinema, a non-functioning hammam, or even some abandoned industrial street. All these "non-spaces" made to pump with life, emotions, sexualities, and *all* of this under the guise of the dark. The visiting queer "it" understands the critical nature of its act, for an "act" needs to always happen *before* a "bust", before someone comes in, before a relative sees, before the wife calls, before another light comes, before the *neighbor* hears something etc. Via the sanctioning of the prohibited, the *sterile* society is created, thereby controlling what one *consume*s and controlling the *consumption* of queerness.

In Japan, you need prescription to chew gum. In Lebanon, "It" (the queer) needs to hide in the shadows to chew "queerness", or it can chew it in public, and risk losing its teeth. The Aristotelian *function* of teeth is to chew and consume. *If* the queer *loses* its teeth to chew *that* which *sustains* it, it either *dies,* or sustains itself on *something* else: *that* which society can offer, *that* with which *new milk teeth* will grow to *chew* and the *old teeth* become obsolete and fall out.

The body always gets rid of its obsolete organs. If there is even a *single* old tooth left there as a reminder of what queerness *used* to taste like, the body will "finish off" society's job in erasing whatever was left of its queer traces. The old queer teeth are the body's appendix and the queer body evolved *beyond* them *into* a new set of teeth, excellent at gnashing and consuming hetero-normativity. Consuming hetero-normativity for *sustenance* is the perfect embodiment of surviving and evolving as queer in Arab waters.

"Arab men often get married young. If having hints of "the monster" at a young age, the family makes sure to marry them even younger"

-Walid, Saudi Arabia, 42

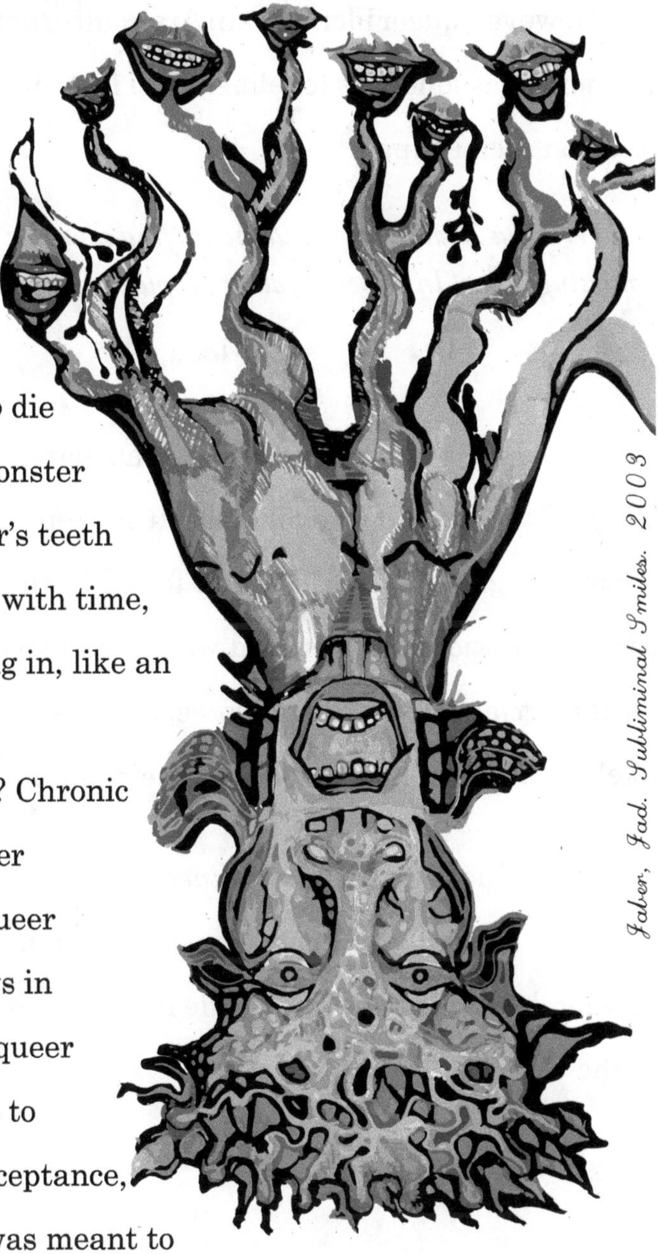

Seen here is a cultural ritual of aborting the queer monster *before* it develops a soul. With time, the queer's old teeth *do* die out, but *not* that monster *inside*. The monster's teeth simply get sharper with time, and they start to dig in, like an ingrown nail.

The symptoms? Chronic anxiety and a deeper perversion of the queer monster, as it grows in the shadows. The queer instinct was meant to *sustain* itself on acceptance, love, and light. It was meant to grow in the *covenant* of the "closeness" of Arab culture, in the safety of the *neighbor*'s backyard, and in the encompassing nature of tightly knitted families.

Faber, Fad. Subliminal Smiles. 2003

95

However, queer identities in Arab culture often find themselves in anomie, as lonely as loneliness can feel, in a culture that prides itself on social support.

"With us Arabs, you would never find an older person aging in a nursing home! In America, older people die alone; their cats eat them!"

-Mona, 61

As being born *by* and *unto* Arab parents, the queer *black sheep* of the Arab household lacks the stepping stone of "leaving home at eighteen", as it is often found in the West. It is against Arabic traditions for men and women to leave their family home *until* marriage. Even *after* divorce, newly single individuals, most likely to be women[xxvi], go back to their familial home.

Arab queer fate is *intertwined* with that of its culture. None of that "coming of age", rite of passage, leaving home, discovering new lands that is found alongside independent identity formation in the west.

---

xxvi In Arab Islamic culture, the man can have more than one wife. It is also more socially permissible for men to have mistresses, thereby increasing their chances of marrying the mistress after divorce. After divorce, men have a larger social and public forum to meet women, while women have a smaller, more privatized forum to meet men. Empowered divorced women are seen as a threat to Arab society's most valued institution: heteronormative marriage. They are seen as threatening by other women, in fear that they can seduce their husbands.

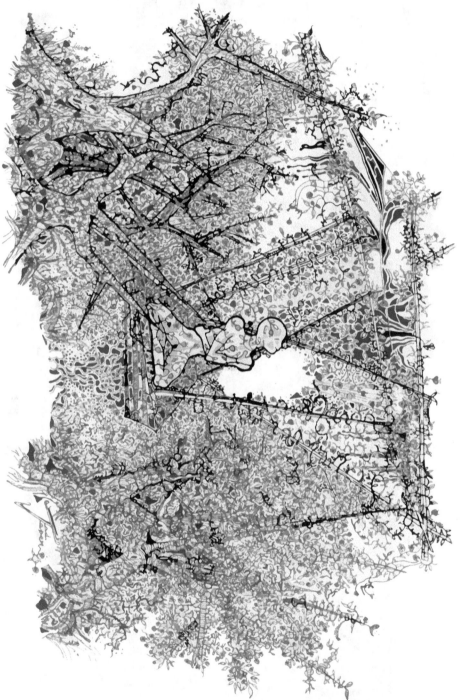

Faber, Jad. In My Garden of Secrets. 2008

11

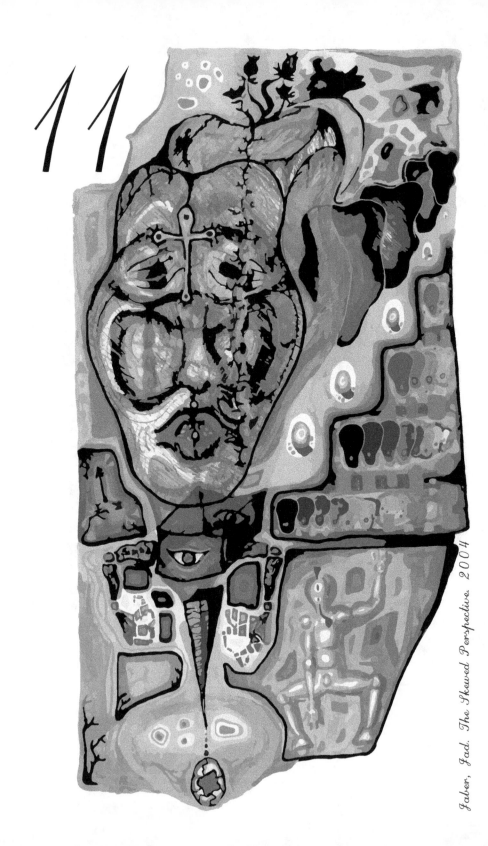

Faber, Jad. The Skewed Perspective. 2004

QUEER

MIGRATION

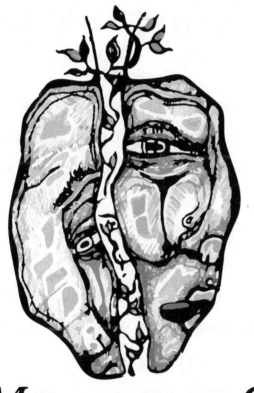

THE MOVEMENT OF QUEER

ESSENCE INTO ARAB

SOCIETY

CHAPTER ELEVEN

Queer Migration: Movement of the Queer Essence Into Arab Society

In the Arab world, young people migrate either to the city, or to the gulf countries "to make money". The migration of their queer identities into maturation though, is met with obstruction and violence.

Most of the queer identities die at sea, before reaching the shore.

As other heteronormative subjectivities migrate into adulthood and completion, queer Arab identities hibernate into absolution in their parents' homes, under the guise of the family, and the holiness of the faith and the father.

It is in these contested spaces of *illusions* and confusion, of family *and* enemy, of neighbor *and* stranger, where the queer identity develops and where it learns the queer language.

It is also in these spaces that the queer experiences the *range* of *conflicted* emotions that come with being queer in the closeness of an Arab home. Emotions such as pride *and* shame, safety *and* fear, calmness *and* anxiety, as well as acceptance *and* judgment.

Similar to an abusive parent or lover, these spaces plague and quarantine queerness, as much as they *nourish* them. To understand the inside perspective of Arab culture is to have the firsthand experience of the queer harem and Arab queerness, basking in the glorious perversions of being a public secret. The queer's existence is forbidden. The term "Forbidden"...

How *essentially* Arab?

The queer harem is an existing *yet* non-existing space: *that* mystery, *that* monster is *also* the *symbol* of the colossal barrier that *divides* the public from the private in the Arab world. It is a bottomless crack in the perfect Arab veneer that holds *all* its truths.

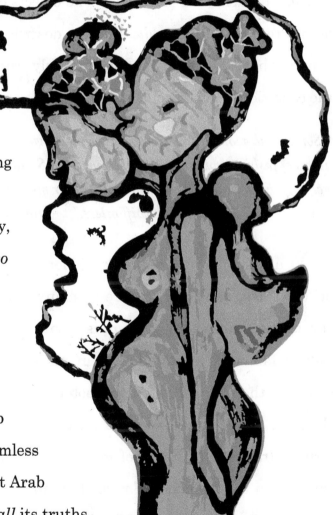

We are *very* particular about our public, versus our private, and even *more* hysterical about the shady space in between. That dichotomy transcends into everything *else* that is Arab: What u see in public, is *never* a reflection of the private: The sold-out Louis Vuiton stores in Paris by gulf consumers do not represent the *same* women who go back home to the gulf, where they are veiled, "hidden" and privatized. The objects consumed *privately* do not represent the *public* subjects described. The conditioned way in which the objects *can* be privately "consumed" resembles the conditioned agency of the subject.

"Some Arab women will purchase the most lavish, extravagant, daring items of fashion, where they will be worn in Saudi, in private all female get-togethers, in secretive affairs with other men or women, or hung and exhibited in glass chiffoniers." -Dina, Kuwait, 35

We are the "Garden of the Forbidden", the *real* queer military of "don't ask, don't tell", where so many prospects of living are sanctioned, and wherever *there* is a sanction, *there* are private/ hidden latencies *mostly* "laced" in pleasure. The *stronger* the sanction, the *stronger* and more rooted the *latencies* become, and the more *intense* the associated pleasure. The latency itself is a form of *truth*, and *a* truth of *many* other truths. The potential *inherent* in the dialectics of revelation and concealment and the *seduction* that goes with the "Garden of the Forbidden" are ample.

102

The *pleasure* is ample. This is the slave's enjoyment of the prohibited in the master's ignorance; this is what falls into the realm of the "more than pleasure" (Zizek, 2006).

Jaber, Jad. The Other Within. 2004

*"I am Syrian, but my friend is German. We come to Beirut in summer.
He loves the sex with Arab boys. He is not afraid to go to local
neighborhoods. He says people like him because he is blond, but has a
beard."* -Ghassan, 38

One notes that it is not just the *creation* of the prohibitions, but the prohibitions *themselves* that become prohibited *to say*, and consequently to *perceive*. An example would be *to say* what is prohibited, which becomes extremely prohibited, even *more* than the prohibition itself! In dictatorships, it is prohibited to say something negative about the ruling dictator. It is even *more* prohibited to say that it *is* prohibited to say something negative about the dictator. Therefore, no one says anything. The prohibitions become *un-announce-able* and the pretension of ignorance becomes *reality*. Violating the implicit versus the explicit rules produce very different cultural consequences...

I will explain this concept using some cultural examples. An Arab women expects her husband to show respect to her publically, represent her socially as his partner in social events, and assure that she is "well taken care of" financially: These are all explicit cultural rules. If you break the explicit rules, this produces gossip, loss of reputation, and a social "witch-hunt". On the other hand, if you maintain the explicit rules, you are able to *tamper* with the implicit rules, one of which, in the example of heteronormative Arab relationships, is monogamy.

104

Arab men *can* cheat, as long as society does not *know*. That *precedes* the importance of his wife *knowing*. In most cases, Arab women *accept* this behavior in men, as part of their nature, *as long as* society does not know. She accepts the breaking of the implicit rules, as long as the explicit rules are held intact. Inversely, an Arab women has more freedom in tampering with implicit rules, such as making more money or having more power than her husband, *as long as* she appears to society as being *his* woman first, succumbing to *his* will, and being "home and family" oriented, which includes managing the feminized labor of the house, and being a "good, present, Arab mother" to her kids and *his* home.Let us look at an example concerning queer culture: A queer Arab can silently and discreetly exist and live out its sexuality. *But* if "it" were to stand on top of an Arab hill and **proclaim:**

"I understand and accept culture's ignorant approach to homosexuality.

I understand the necessary need to alter my behavior as to be accepted by the world around. And I have done these concessions.

My sexual identity is not public.

My sexual life is private.

My behavior is hetero-normative and I will marry a woman.

...I do identify as gay, though..."

Due to that *last* closing statetment and the *public* admittance of queerness, "it" would no longer be *allowed* to live out its sexuality, no matter how repressed, contained, closeted, hidden or compacted.

If "it" were to **proclaim:**

> *"I will be the archetype of the hyper masculine Arab man, make money, have children...but feel gay..."*

"It" would *still* not be allowed to exist because people would *know*, and in *knowing your truth*, Arab culture can no longer host you. More over, by *voicing and representing* queerness, the queer has desecrated the *explicit rules* of Arab culture.

Voicing truths in general is something frowned upon in the Arab world, and is a form of breaking explicit rules. Voicing that Arab culture frowns upon voicing the truth is even more frowned upon.

"The secret", in general, exists in the space where the explicit rules are respected, but the implicit ones can be manipulated with. But the implicit tampering needs to *stay* implicit. In terms of the Arab queer, *that* tampering is happening in the deepest fibers of Arab culture.

The queer needs to understand the positive and necessary connotation of its tampering. "It" was created by Arab culture *to* tamper, and unlike what it has been *taught* by society, it is not tampering with the holy, normal, *natural*, eternal Arab essence, because the Arab essence *is* essentially queer, and *has* a queer history. The illusion that there exists this homogeneous heteronormative category of "normal Arabs" that the queer *should* fit into is unrealistic and reductionist.

As modern Arabs often voice *their disgust* over acts of "queer tampering", they should know that *disgust* is an extreme, *reactive* emotion. Usually, people react aggressively to what they disdain. They also tend to disdain either that which they recognize in themselves within other people, or that which they want in others, but cannot have.

Nothing so promotes the growth of consciousness as [the] inner confrontation of opposites (Carl Jung; Memories, Dreams and Reflections; Page 345).

I have firmly come to believe that Arab culture fears and disdains the growth of its population's consciousness, because that creates the *ability* for the masses to question their cultural and religious systems. Queerness promotes the growth of Arab consciousness and is sanctioned accordingly.

"It took a radically different queer experience to bring out the queer subject in myself and it takes a radically queer experience to bring out the queer subject in Arab society. but it is right there, lurking to get out.." - Adham, 27, Lebanon

Jaber, Jad. The Masked Self. 2011

12

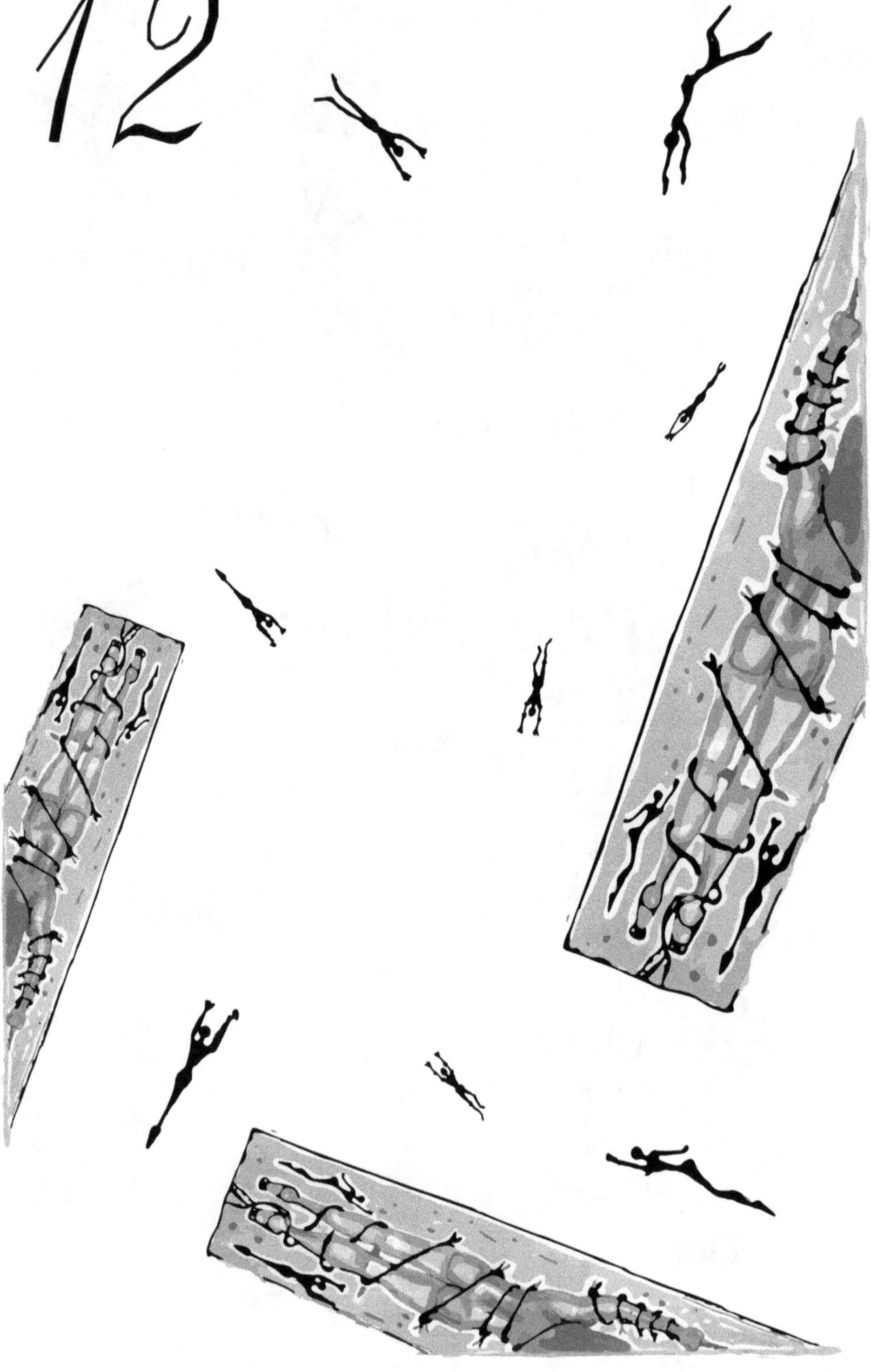

THE QUEER GYM
ETHNOGRAPHY

Faber, Fad. New York. 2004

CHAPTER TWELVE

The Queer Gym Ethnography

I knew of sustenance, secrets and fears of being "outed"...

I knew of hidden expressions... of the fear of annihilation with a kiss, a hold of the hand, or a *queer* stare...

Maybe the sexual identities I experienced in New York City, were *the subjects*, the *real* "he's".

But my ability to find pleasure in them, *without* the sanctions, had been *martyred* with my Arab queerness. The secrecy of the closet has offered me a space for an unconventional Eros to proliferate (Secomb 2007Ed) and as a queer Arab, I *worry* about what has *flourished* within me.

As a young Arab "It" living for a few years in New York, what I had most yearned for, as Queer, was the freedom in sexual liberality and in being a *sexual* being. I yearned to express my "it"-ness, being that *it* had been repressed during my previous years in Arab countries.

Opposing that previous described "harem" was the *extrovertly* gay-friendly New York City gym I was training in at the time. The men there where *explicitly* forward in their sexual approach, showing *all* their queer feathers, and I could only *feel* the over-taste and the *over-stench* of human sexuality.

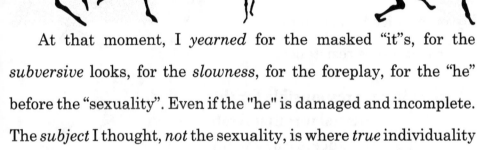

At that moment, I *yearned* for the masked "it"s, for the *subversive* looks, for the *slowness*, for the foreplay, for the "he" before the "sexuality". Even if the "he" is damaged and incomplete. The *subject* I thought, *not* the sexuality, is where *true* individuality exists.

But I came from a place where the queer subject *is* a dead object produced by Arab society.

I came from a place where *subject* and *sexuality* are separated by years of public versus private.

How can this *symbiotic merge* I see in my New York City gym make sense to my eyes?

How can I possibly be permeable to this representation?

I knew of no Arab queer "I's", of no extroverted Loves.

How could I *identify* what makes a queer subject?

Looking retrospectively at the New York gym experience, I did not *know* if this was a case of "you *can* take the queer *out* of the Arab (world), but you *can't* take the Arab *out* of the queer". I did not *know* if my queerness had been tainted by Arab emotions of "shame", "exposed", and "public", for what *felt* wrong with showing your queer feathers, should have felt *right*.

My internalized reaction to queer feathers is resistance.

Arab culture is responsible for this internal war that Arab queers carry within them, regardless of where their souls and bodies migrate.

"His hand touched my hand in the back of the cab, and I just automatically pulled it away. Looking left and right, had anyone seen? My heart was beating, and I was in fight or flight mode. He placed his hand on my hand again, and bent his head forward saying, "Don't worry, you're no longer home"".

-Rami, Lebanon, on experiencing internalized resistance to queer behavior after migrating to the USA from the Arab World.

The subjects I knew were *all* "it"s, and so I could *pinpoint* an internalized resistance in myself *to* "*complete* queer subjects".

If *this* is what *I* internalized, I could not imagine what *other* Arab queers had internalized: other Arab queers who had *less* access to knowledge, love and acceptance.

With what I had internalized, I *felt* as an imposter in the *country of queerness*, a county I always thought I *naturally* belonged to. *Yes*, I had *resisted* the Arab indoctrination, but I was also *simultaneously* rehabilitated to find identity and pleasure in "incomplete queer subjects", and I believe this is a source of *violence* in queer Arab relationships.

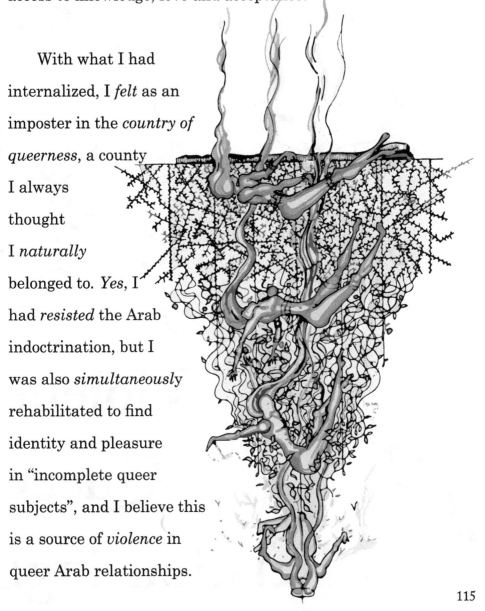

13

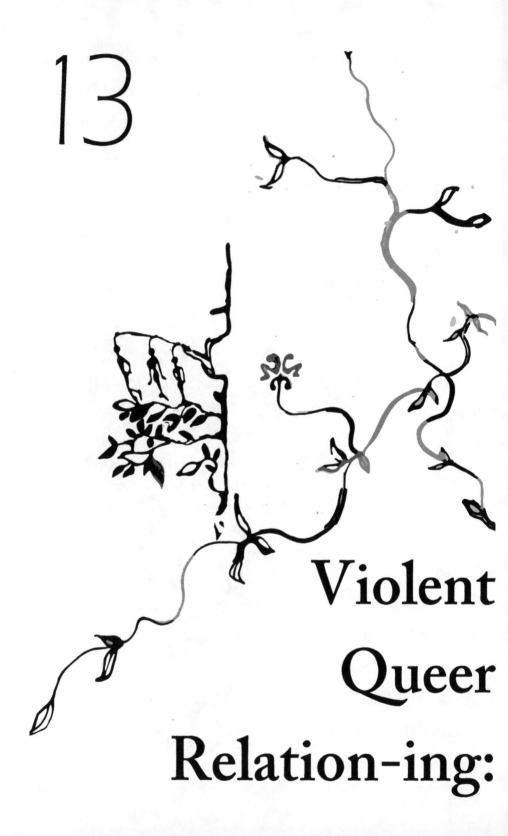

Violent
Queer
Relation-ing:

Jaber, Jad. *Cocaine Heart.* 2015

Are Arabs Queer Relationships More Violent?

CHAPTER THIRTEEN

Violent Queer Relation-ing: Are Arabs Queer Relationships More Violent?

"I never felt loved in my queer relationships at home (Lebanon). I felt I could not love either. Seeing him properly and having sex had to happen in his parent's mountain home when they are in the city. It had to happen fast, because his sisters and kids came up often. In summer, his parents would stay up in the mountain house so we could not see each other privately for weeks. He would complain that I am unloving, but I always felt anxious when he touched my hands in the car, or when he wanted to kiss in the elevator: what if one of the neighbors saw! They would kill me!"

- Wael, Lebanon, 25

"Incomplete queer subjects", offered completeness in the small claustrophobic spaces of Arab heteronormative culture, including the spaces of a relationship, where admittance to a queer relationship or a physical show of "relation-ing" is met with extreme cultural aggression. Queers have to relation *silently*.

118

Two, *fractional* individuals attempt at finding *unity* in the *framework of love*, but also in the interplay of fear, hiding, and anxiety within Arab culture. Similar to a bald eagle mating ritual, completeness and wholeness is sought after, accompanied with what emotionally feels like "freefalling from the clouds in a death spiral". As Arab queers experience *themselves* in the confinement of a cultural closet, Arab relationships actualize in the confinement of a *slightly* larger closet.

Primarily, *that* space, is not enough to house the *largeness of love*, which includes the need to develop as a recognized couple, engage in recreational events, form intricate partnerships, adopt children, and gain public recognition etc. Second, the relationship itself becomes *that* fleeting *event* of queerness, like a quick car sex session, rooted in extreme emotions that eventually translate in real-life time into jealousy, *possessiveness,* conflict, violence and strained communication. It is the queer *moment* that the Arab queer is trying to *possess*, not the queer *person*.

The kernel of all jealousy is the *lack of love* (Carl Jung; Memories, Dreams and Reflections) or the lack of *space to love*, fully. Queers may experience love but may not experience *living it out*, *acting it out*, *performing it through*, therefor deeply *feeling* it. Relationships *feel* to queer Arabs *as if* they lack love, and they *do*. Queer hearts *can* encompass a lot more love, and the queer spirit *can* experience absoluteness in relation-ing.

To overcompensate for that *lack*, other binding and passionate emotions are introduced into the dynamics of the relationship to *mimic* completeness. Jealousy is definitely one of these emotions, and jealousy leads to violence. The relationships then come in the form of Arab queer events: a series of incomplete, emotional, beautiful, violent events. The groundwork laid ahead, for these "queer events" to *consistently occur*, is simply Arab culture. Arab culture's anti-queer discourse concerning the perversion of queer culture is ludicrous, once one is aware that the *restraints* it has placed on queer culture *are* the cause of its perversion.

Jaber, Jad. Seeded. 2016

It is Arab culture's heteronormative perversions and fetishes that are setting the queer discourse at this point in history.

Jaber, Jad. The Rabbit Hole. 2005

14

ICKY, STICKY, QUEER SEX

Icky, Sticky, Queer Sex

As queer Arab events are rarely described, while queer theorists have *overplayed* sexuality and identity, introducing the notions of the public secret and hidden pleasures *into* day-to-day queer sex, has had its effects: namely, *increased* perversion and *increased* intensity. The secret (or truth) of queer theory is that it does not want to talk or represent queer sex. Queer theory does not—despite what it tells itself— like the icky, sticky, and yucky. It needs to carefully mop up the messy, the dirty, and the sexually *disgusting* (Dollimore). In order to remain squeaky clean it has to cast out that which it deems *too* perverse. (O'Rourke, 2014). *Negotiating down* sex and pleasure seems to be a common denominator in *all* queer cultures, including Arab queer culture.

The public secret of Arab queerness has made it perverse *enough* to be expelled from Arab culture. Nowhere, can you find the "icky, sticky, and yucky" representation of queer sex, even though in countries like Lebanon, hyper sexualization is *often* represented, but in the bodies of women.

Representing *carnal* queer sex is probably the *ultimate* sin in Arab culture and even more sinful than the act of queerness itself, because it *grounds* the queer act and *details* it, proving that queerness is not woven from the fictions of queer minds, but is a reality of Arab existence and part of the Arab social fabric.

"A single Sexual experience back home was more intense than four years of gay sex in London! I describe it as my face pressed on my childhood neighbor's backdoor, his mother still in the house! Had anyone heard, they would have cut out my genitals. It was the most silent and soul-shaking orgasm I had felt"

-Saif, 24, Iraq, on experiencing queer sex after coming back to the Arab world from Europe.

Re-archiving Arab history of queerness, takes collecting the perversions, fetishes, narratives, and sex from *all* the queer subjects, to *translate* an *oral tradition* of queer existence, a tradition of whispers and secrets that echo as loud as Arab hetero-normalization itself, *into* palpable, visual, linguistic, and colorful archives.

What does the history of sex look like without evidence of sexual identities or proof that sex acts occurred? How might an analysis of gossip, rumors, and perhaps lies about sex help us to write political history? (Potter, 2006)

"I'm outwardly feminine (na3em) and have been so since I was born. I make no exceptions at home. But I would never tell my family I am gay, or talk about being gay with any family member.
Khalijis prohibit gays, but also accept and want soft and feminine men. It wasn't always "un-sayable". In my grandfather's generation, they used to call it for what it is, a man who likes boys (bi7ib el sobyan).
Now it is not said.
Old Kuwaiti theatre plays also had many outwardly gay people. Even though, if you walk now in a mall in Kuwait, you would find so much more metro-sexuality and androgyny than before, but most people, like my mother's generation, are actually becoming more close-minded and against being gay."

-Fayzan, Kuwait, 32

The modern queer archive should reconnect all the historical queer events erased by the modern history of religious extremism, gender segregation, and Arab conservatism, to paint the "full queer subject", including its icky, sticky sex.

Faber, Fad. Oriental Orgy. 2009

15

ARAB QUEER'S METAMORPHOSIS

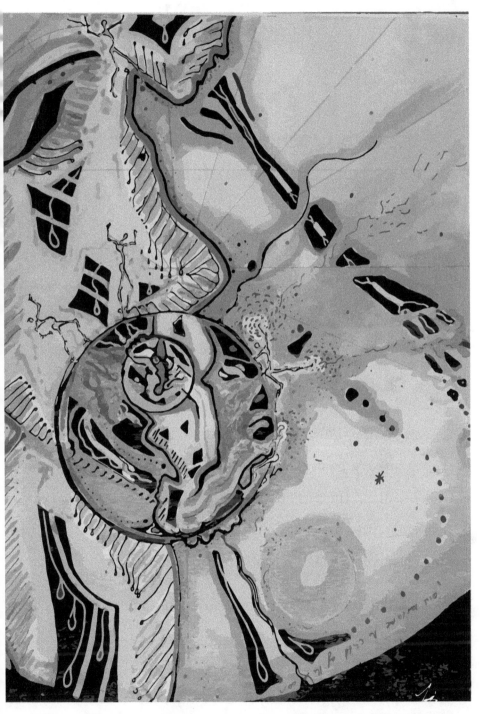

& *Its Congenital Birth*

Arab Queer's Metamorphosis
And Congenital Birth

In every adult, there lurks an *eternal child,* something that is always becoming, is never completed, and calls for unceasing care, attention, and education. That is the part of the personality which wants to develop and become whole.(C. G. Jung, 1964).

To anatomize Queer Development, Nietzsche's (Nietzsche, Thus Spoke Zarathustra) Parable of the Three Metamorphosis *depicts* the Arab queer's past, present and *possibly* future. This parable entices beautiful images and language telling the story of a *camel* that morphs into a *lion,* then to a *newborn child*, as it *migrates* from society and civilization *into* to the wilderness.

How can this story be *parallelized* to queer Arab development?

Arab queers begin in the Camel stage, the *heaviest* stage for the soul, where the queers are renounced as "beasts of burden".

In this stage, they nod and smile as they bend over to be saddled.

How Arab is the queer camel, saddled by society's norms and values, and appearances?

In this stage, the queer persists and resists, as society's prey until it cannot *bear* anymore and thus it creates the intention of breaking the bonds of slavery embedded in social requirements and dogma. The queer loves those that despise it, and *helps* that which frightens it.

It *is* a *hungry* spirit, but *hungry for falseness*, because it *avoids* truth and *avoids* knowledge. Truth and knowledge *cannot* be experienced in a culture that glorifies closeted and contained queerness. In its camel-ness, it is formidable to even *seek* the new, to even (idea)lise any new event or possibility.

Yes, Arab queers, generally closeted, maintain their sense of pride and acceptance, *but on the expense of what*? Its wisdom! It gains its short-term social triumphs, namely conditioned acceptance and timid tolerance, *but on the expense of what*? Its long-term survival! It *lacks* loyalty to its cause, because it *lacks* its *own* cause. Its cause is *society's* cause.

As the camel, the queer is purely the product of society's conditioning, nurturing and demands. From an insider's perspective, it is impossible to *notice* the structure of society, as you are *part* of it and too involved abiding by its responsibilities, duties, and values.

As the camel moves towards the wilderness, the second stage begins: The *camel* morphs into *Lion*. To Revolt and destroy, to refuse and refute, to disobey, and to be unreasonable is to *become the lion.*

This results in the ability to finally reach a total state of chaos and destruction, and thus entropy. A blank state where all false idols are demolished and invalidated, and *now* the Lion can give way to *newness.*

The wild and untamed lion is free and sovereign and is the *lord of his lord-ness.*

He is hostile to whatever attempts to control it.

He functions from his will, not from the *will of society...*

That which is described to be as *unscripted in unyielding glittering gold...*

That which claims to be the holder of a thousand years of values and beliefs created...

That of which all that *is* created has *already been* created.

This stage of the lion depicts a struggle for victory, against an over-arching and an unyielding system. The purpose of the lion is to *create* new values, which the lion *lacks* the *potential* to create. But it creates, more importantly, the freedom *for* creating.

The lion *assumes* new rights, new values, and creates the *fertile space* for the *child* to be born into. The lion finally sees the fallacies and arbitrariness in everything, which is cemented and holy in culture, transforming into the final stage of Nietzsche's parable, the *newborn child*.

The last stage of the *newborn child* depicts the soul's ability to create his or her own rules and notions to live by. One would ask what *could* the child *do* that the lion *cannot?* The child can forget! Through the pure power of innocence, the child can forget its previous inscriptions; the fears, shame, and meanings internalized as the limits of adult thinking, feeling and behaving. The child can make new beginnings, creating newness, creating "first movements", creating "creations", and creating life for a new subjectivity, and therefor fate. Hence the child lives in its *own* world, according to its *own* will. *It is the welcomed outcast.*

After the camel stage, where *does* the Arab queer go? The Arab Queer in reality *exists* at the stage of the Camel. Its spiritual development stopped, because it lacks, at times the intention, but mostly the senses and skills to progress towards it. With its subvert acts of revolt, the Arab queer *thinks* itself to *be* the child, but in essence, *reiterates* the *same* pillars with which its daily saddling, as a salivating *camel*, was *made* possible.

The Arab Queer *omits* the Lion stage...

There are *no* lions in the queer Arab world, only prideful *pussycats* with artificial manes roaring when all they *really* want to do is *purr*.

One *can* hope that the queer fate is a case of *rolling out* of its center, versus *convulsing back into* its center, until it dots out unto disappearance.

Queer society is victim of society but also victim of its own *joy* of *being* slave and thus *free* of responsibility: free to hide in the shadows and let a very socially awkward sexual mayhem take place in a community where the very term *gay* as happy takes on a *double* entendre: gay *is* happy, but *also* happy to be the victim of society, happy to enjoy the *lashes* of the social dogmatic whips... for *in it* they have found a freedom of being free and complete adults: adult *camels.*

This is not to say that the fight for queer rights is utterly non-existent, but the Arab world's norms, rituals and values even destroyed *heterosexuality*, by using *sex* as the weapon to oppress and subjugate, reminiscent of the fourteenth century church of the dark ages; sex as prohibition, sex as shame, but sex *also* as hidden pleasure.

During the recent Arab spring, also referred to as a time of revolution of queer thought and behavior, the space for change, for the *lion stage,* was *almost* created. Unfortunately, Arab Islamic authorities made sure to violently suppress the queer outbreak into oblivion, and the *old system* was simultaneously reinvigorated, and pushed *back* towards conservatism.

The frontward movement from the Arabian desert to the freedom of the wildernes is going to take a coalition and a pride 'pun intended' of queer lions.

Unfortunately, Arab queers who *wanted* to look front, could *only* look back, and what they saw, was unfortunately, their *future*.

> *"For me, if you're not privileged, powerful, connected, or rich enough (as an Arab queer) to cause change, you become the victim of non-change. If you are that victim, I say, get out, and come back when you can cause change. The life of that victim isn't worth it."*
>
> – Jonathan, 33, Lebanon

Jaber, Jad. Mine, Moon. 2018

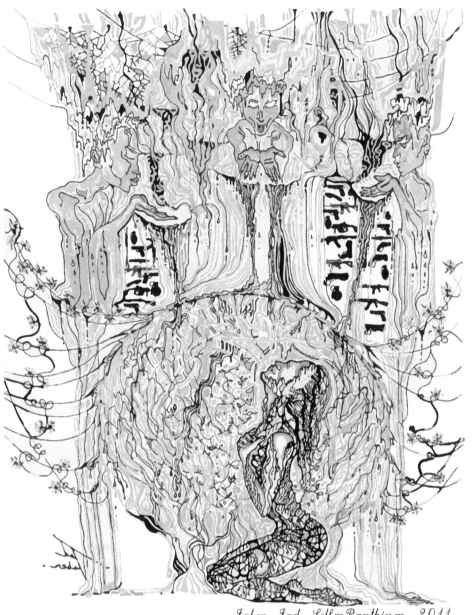

Jaber, Jad. Self-Panthiesm. 2011

"IT'S" A QUEER

WAR

"It's" a Queer War

On June 2015, news of the legalization of gay marriage in the US was hitting the Middle East. Social media newsfeeds in Lebanon, Syria, Iraq and Jordan were buzzing with a *war*: a war between "Rainbow flags" and its "Arab opposition", opposing more so the *Arab expression of queerness*, rather than the message of queerness *itself*, which was being expressed as a global support of gay marriage.

That right there is the field of war in which the queer phenomenon exists: the field of Arab *reactions* to queerness.

It is in the nature of political bodies always to see the evil in the opposite group, just as the individual has an ineradicable tendency to get rid of everything he does not know and does not want to know about himself by foisting it off on somebody else (Carl Jung; The Undiscovered Self).

"Being queer is a criminal offence against humanity, and admitting to it, is an even bigger crime. These sick individuals should be rehabilitated and quarantined in special centers in remote and secluded locations. We all have children we love and are afraid for them. The reason queers exist is the family's inability to raise its children correctly and the encouraging western-influenced environment for queer sickness"

- @ANAEnsaaaaan, April 14 2018, Arab reactions to queer online representation

Why Arabs *themselves* emotionally react to queerness is something I am sure *they* are unaware of. The psyche does not *merely* react. It gives its own specific answer to the influences at work upon it. (Jung,1961) Arabs' reaction *towards* queers is, *in reality*, a reaction to the queer existing *within* them.

Through *gendered* spaces like harems, *gendered* rituals like funerals, and *gendered* social institutions like schools, Arabs have created spaces for queer thoughts to come to life, but also to become perverted and grow in the shadows. The reaction they have towards queer representation is indicative of the perversions that has grown in *their* shadows and *their* fear of its coming to light. *As* they push the queer subjects *out*, they push their queer instinct *in*.

It might be time for Arab heteronormative culture to embrace its queer shadows, as something that has a purpose and a function on two fronts.

The first function is *reasserting* the founding rules and regulations of Arab hetero-normativity. The second, is *reconnecting* Arab hetero-normativity to its libidinal *queer* instinct, with queer in this sense, not necessarily meaning gay or lesbian, but *different* and *individual*. Arab culture has created vacuums between identities, and their corresponding fetishes, libidos and instincts. Collectivity does not have to entail the *death of individualities*.

"You are spreading corruption in Arab societies and these queers deserted their religion, society, honor and traditions, and became lonely and castaways. They do not belong to any society, and their identity hallucination will cause them to commit suicide the way Freddy Mercury and George Michael did, because they have severe internal struggles"

-@ouchaouau, April 2018, Arab reactions to queer online representation

Objects of queerness have been scarcely represented in the Arab world, while *subjects of queerness* in modern Arab history have been pushed to oblivion. The importance of representation and in having living, speaking, subjects with names, ethnicities, voices and backgrounds is exemplified in the Arabic video[xxvii] and campaign, #NoLongerAlone, which was shared widely on Facebook. It was one of the first holsitic representations of queer Arab subjects. The War-ground of queer existence in the Arab world peeps its violent images and languages through the safety and ambiguity of social media and twitter.

[xxvii] https://www.facebook.com/afemena.org/videos

Not that the perpetrators are attempting to *be* ambiguous, since Arab society condones and promotes queer violence.

"How does discussing all the violent acts against Arab queers help queers in getting rehabilitated into normal people? Showcasing them as such in the norms of society causes shame to them and their families. Imagine how their fathers feel!?"

- @aboodib, April 14 2018, Arab reactions to queer online representation

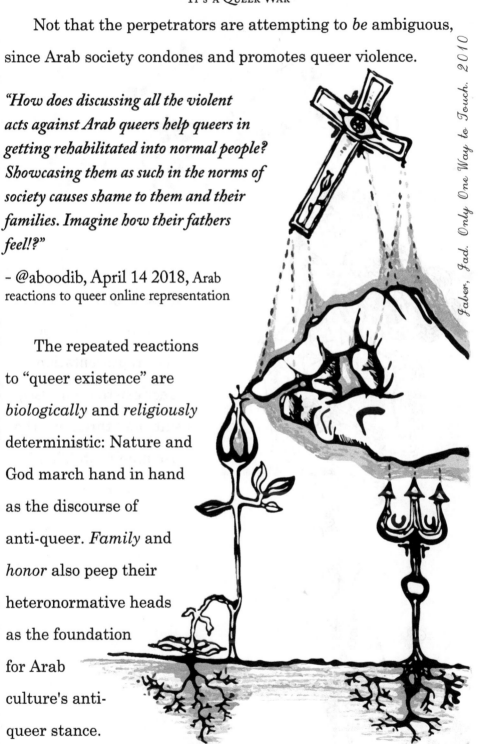

Faber, Fad. Only One Way to Touch. 2010

The repeated reactions to "queer existence" are *biologically* and *religiously* deterministic: Nature and God march hand in hand as the discourse of anti-queer. *Family* and *honor* also peep their heteronormative heads as the foundation for Arab culture's anti-queer stance.

Queers appear to shame *everything* they touch. The representation of queer existence in *itself* insults and threatens the masculine Arab-Islamic identity.

*"My father was a calm man. I never heard him scream or
lay a hand on my sisters or me.
I hid my queerness as long as possible.
One night, I came back home with bite-marks on my neck.
My mother saw it, told me "I am a woman, and I know
that only a man can do that", and started yelling hysterically
to my father. When I came out to him, my father leapt across
the room towards my neck.
He choked me so hard it took five people to get him of me"*

– Ahmad, 29, Lebanon

Cultural violence attacks all aspects of queer existence,
leaving *nothing* unsaid from public queer behavior to private
acts of sex and fetishism. In war (and love), *all* acts of violence
are permissible. In a culture that stigmatizes sex, acts of war
are more *likely* to take a *sexual* turn.

"Anal openings are for exiting not entering, you dirt!"

-@krmkrm18, April 14 2018, Arab reactions to queer online representation

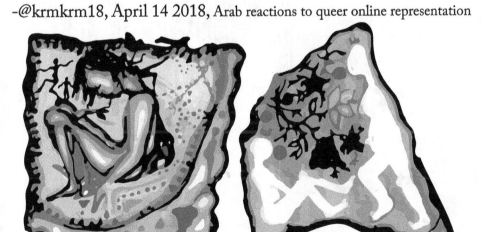

147

17

Faber, Fad. Made of Tears, 2014

TIME TO PAUSE

Time to pause

To move from online wars, to the wars of the queer subject, I would like to focus on myself, as part of The Queer War Generation "Jeel el 7arb".

This particular "It" comes from an even *more* particular history and is also the son-daughter-hermaphrodite of War, a war within both its exterior and interior existence, a *generation* of "It"s, a generation of monstrosities... It is the generation of all-encompassing violence, starting with violence towards the other, and naturally progressing to violence against the self.

I was Born after a twenty year old war that had started in 1975 and ended in 1989, followed by another war in the early 90's and massive explosions in Beirut in the early 2000's. The situation has been declining ever since in what is now *known* as the Mediterranean crescent of violence (Jordan, Palestine, Syria, Lebanon), which has witnessed Turkish, French and British colonialization (Traboulsi 2007).

This area simply did not *know* peace and neither did *my* parent's generation, nor *their* parents. I have heard quotes that we live in bloodstained lands where *every* grain of earth is stained, and where *every* soul is stained accordingly.

The "It" has yet to *pause*, to find a resting ground, to root *down*, to look *up*, to understand its trajectory and ordinances and *exit* the limbo-ic state of negotiated existence. First doing so by de-*god*ifying the divine rules, rites, and institutions imposed on the individual by external powers that become internalized in its systems of beliefs and feelings (Agamben, Potentialities: 1999). Man always has some mental reservation *even* in the face of divine decrees. Otherwise, where would be his freedom? What would be the use of that freedom if it could not threaten Him who threatens it? (Carl Jung) Under the threat of destruction, the Arab queer *also* has a chance for freedom. No one can appreciate freedom more than a war-torn Arab queer. No one should be more willing to fight for it, especially those who have *already* martyred parts of themselves.

War has permeated into the queer.

The war of right and wrong, of natural and abnormal, of

hopeful and doomed, of god and the devil, of reality and

delusion, of *right or wrong*, has simply *moved* bodies.

It is now festering in the body of the Arab queer.

The presence of thoughts though, is *more* important than our subjective judgment of them as *right or wrong*. These judgments must not be suppressed, for they also are existent thoughts which are part of our wholeness (Jung, 1964). It is better to have *that* subjective war, then *not* have an internal war *at all*. The queer *is* at war to *retain* their queer thought, even if interplayed between all these antagonistic variables. Those that *aren't* at war have *crossed* the limits of suppressing their queer thought, to *obliterating* it, abdicating their queer sovereignty for that of society's. They have raised their queer white flags!

"Let them paint you as queer. Would you rather not be painted at all ?"

-Ziad, 26, Beirut

18

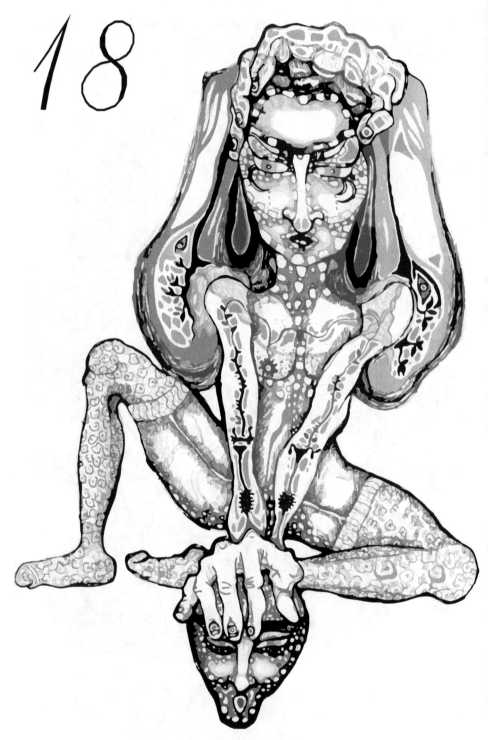

Faber, Jad. The Jilted Bride. 2004

QUEER WAR SEMIOTICS

Jaber, Jad. The Half Blind. 2005

CHAPTER EIGHTEEN

Queer War Semiotics

Let us look at a *semiotic, realistic* and more importantly, *queer* perspective to "war". War *is* a sexual act of *screwing* the other and *screwing* the self with all its phallic symbols and penis-shaped artillery (Carlin 2004). This *national* and *collective* nature to war, translates *locally* to single *individual queer acts*, enacted by the *bodies of war*, namely: soldiers and citizens, masters and slaves, conquerors and the conquered, savors and victims, and other *actors* of fetishized power dynamics. War in *itself* is *queer* in *two* functions. On a *national, collective* and *macroscopic* level, war is queer in its politically autonomous psychotic act of self-preservation. On a *local, individual,* and *microscopic* level, war is queer through socially queer behavior, recorded *vigorously* during history in gendered *sex and war crimes* usually targeting the "colonialized other".

Notoriously *represented* in the Queer behavior of the American Army in Iraq (Burks) as a clear embodiment of the *power* dynamics at hand.

The perceived *power* of *powerful* men over *powerless* men in war has the same sexual nature as that of a *sadist* over a *masochist* in the privacy of the bedroom. Except, the masochist *consents* to the violence. The context of war assigns queer sex to donors and receivers *in alignment* with the power dynamics: the *powerful* inflict violence, and the *disempowered* receive it. War glamorizes emphasized heterosexuality. Strict, aggressive, comparative and competitive, are amongst many characteristics developed within soldiers of war. War is an *over-masculinized* macho act of proving oneself and *hiding* insecurity and identity behind ultra-violence. **War is simply queer, as it does not seek out its heterosexual partner "peace"...** War seeks no "other"... **It seeks out itself...**

War is Arab culture's *real* homosexual, a self-masturbator, self-engrossed; sustaining itself on *sameness,* also meaning "mathli"[xxviii] in Arabic.

As an underdeveloped queer "It", I recall the romanticized, yet "shamed" stories of one of the biggest political groups in Lebanon and their behavior during the Lebanese civil war. Word of mouth, as well as research (McCormick 2006), showed the drug and sex fuelled tactics of this Arabic, christian militia, famous for maiming women through their genitalia, on the metallic fences of their "just-conquered" land.

xxviii   The politically correct for "Gay" in Arabic, is "Mithli", literally translates to "Sameness" or "that of which is attracted to itself".

157

The scenario described before is indicative of a *prevalent* post-war mentality, which allows a tentative (and tacit) exploration of sexual boundaries firmly repressed during combat that remains staunchly patriarchal (Hajj 2014). Hence, on-the-ground queer acts, whether homosexual or heterosexual in nature were as common as the *embodiment* of the queer *spirit* of war and patriarchy: The same *spirit* that sanctions homo-queerness *also* encourages hetero-queerness.The aggressive, masochistic and sadistic nature of the *actions* of the *actors* of war *is* a dark shade of queer, but *nevertheless* a shade of queer... Is one better than the other? Had Arab queers been able to develop healthily and become *full* subjects, I would have easily pointed them as the *right* kind of queer, *knowing* that violent sadomasochistic war criminals are definitely the *wrong* kind of queer. Even the language used to recall the "stories of war": Those saying it and those hearing it were *engulfed* in the *sexual* nature of violence of war as something that tastes *so* good, but is *so* bad for you to pleasure in.

Violence and queerness as described above *merge* into *one* culture and language: the language *of society* then becomes the language *of the mind.* To stick to the *language* of war, the Arab queer has renounced its *sovereignty.* It has renounced its *sovereignty* in the multiple concessions and compromises it does for its survival. Yes, there *is* a land that exists for the Arab Queer.

158

But the inhabitants of a land who have *renounced* their sovereignty are at a pre-given existential disadvantage. They *are* the foreign. They *are* the parasites, living side by side to their host. They are Arab Culture's *"neighbor[xxix]"* and in their parasitism and trespass, they re-create the "proper" behavior of the collective, the manual, the guide. It is via their queer *image* and *language* for "Parasitism comes with an image, and a language" (Ronell) that the "big other" knows what *"not* to see", *"not* to do" and *"not* to say". Arab culture is a powerful "big other", always in affect, pushing those parasitical influences out to the margins. The bigger the crowd, the more negligible the individual (Carl Jung; The Undiscovered Self).

The Queer itself is not sovereign in its *being* as the being of a particular subjectivity presumes its *oneness*. Instead, the non-sovereign queer self is fractured, schizmed, imbalanced, *off the wagon* and it suffers from chronic anxiety. There are different and sometimes antagonistic forms of sovereignty, and it is always in the name of one that one attacks another (Derrida 2001).Can the queer become *the sovereign* if Arab culture was to perceive queerness as being *part* of *its* sovereignty? Or does the queer need to establish its own sovereignty, the sovereignty of the newborn child?

xxix   See Chapter 19 "Fear of the Queer Neighbor".

To understand this "war between sovereignties", one should bring to light the only *real* sovereign in Arab culture: the Arab male archetype[xxx]. Many of Arab society's reactions towards queerness are *less* in reference to the queer nature, as they are for the accentuation of society's emphasized heteronormativity embodied in *that* Arab archetype. A cemented archetype upon which gendered hierarchies are built, world views are proven right, and status-quo's are kept in their place.

"In Lebanon, You cannot be Palestian, Syrian, colored, female, queer, or many other similar categories, if you were to maintain your social status. Arabs are the worst towards each other.yet paradoxially in awe of foreigness. but we can discriminate against you for almost anything"

-Jameel, 47, Lebanon

Society and its sovereign archetypal hero can *not* forgo the queer's development for it is in the name of their *own* development that the queer is attacked and martyred, depicting an antagonistic relationship that *keeps* the sacred definition of the heterosexual sovereign unscathed. The Lebanese queer has been pumped blind by the aforementioned *discourse of War*. Placed within its singular body, are its queer nature *and* its antidote, the overtly heterosexual nature of war.

xxx   Carl Jung was one of the first to use "archetype" in his theory of the human psyche. He believed that universal, mythic characters—archetypes—reside within the **collective unconscious** of people. Archetypes differ by culture and history, but they encompass a wide range of common characteristics associated with one subject; examples of such archetypes would be the father, the mother, the child, the old man, and now, "The Queer Arab".

That catabolic mix they create resembles another *Yin-Yang* arabesque relationship to queerness: often like the tides constantly pushing or pulling, but never both simultaneously and never neither. While the relationship between Arabs and queers *seems* clear to *both* the foreign gaze and to Arabs themselves, the dynamics at hand are more complex than "Arabs don't have gays".

Suffering from painful *phantom Limb* symptoms[xxxi], and unable to medicate, express or name the symptoms to the *outside* world, they continue to *sense* that queer tongue they lost in the *first* war of childhood, that queer soul that was severed in the *second* war of teenage-hood, and that queer agency, amputated in the *last* war of adulthood.

QUEERNESS HAS BEEN CONTAINED

TO AN OBJECT LACKING A SUBJECT

TO A TAG OF UNKNOWN/ UNNAMABLE

AND TO AN EVENT.

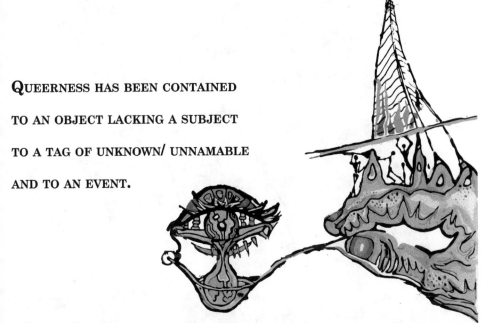

xxxi   Phantom Limb: is the sensation felt by amputees that an amputated or missing limb is *still* attached. Up to eighty percent of amputees experience phantom sensations, with the majority of sensations being painful.

19

Jaber, Jad. Destruction by Exploration. 2006

FEAR OF THE
QUEER NEIGHBOR

Fear of the Queer Neighbor: The Anxious Queer Phallus

An Arab walks into their home, their front door slightly hinged. As they look inside anxiously and fearfully, thinking of the identity of the trespasser, they start to imagine the scenarios:

Is it that stranger who was waiting by the pavement last night?

Is it that robber the local news spoke about?

Might it be that foreign worker who came a month ago to fix the electricity? As they walk inward towards the room, the horror they saw, was more than they could ever imagine.

It was their neighbor!

Inspired by Zizek's lecture[xxxii], the fear of the queer neighbor[xxxiii] is best explained as the most violent form of trespass and transgression a queer Arab subject can experience. The added point here is that this fear seems to increase, the more collective the culture is.

xxxii   European Graduate School, August 2014
xxxiii   The queer Arab *neighbor* can be anything from the queer's mother, cousin, neighbor, friend, or acquaintance, but most violently, the neighbor can be "the self", *that* "other" within the self. The symptoms of that fractured state are chronic anxiety, as well as the propensity to make wrong and self-harming choices.

Arab culture is *extremely* collective exemplified by the strong barrier between the public and the private, the notion of honor and shame, and the power of *reputations* in determining individual fates.

Arab culture prides itself on collective cultural values such as hospitality and *closeness* but behaves *inversely* when it comes to the dynamics of the *queer subject* and *the neighbor*.

The closer *the neighbor* to the queer *subject*, the more there is a *fear of closeness*.

"When I got on Grindr, the first thing I did was block any profile closer than 50 meters... I always try to contact the person furthest from my location"

Ali, 24, Beirut

The neighbor is that who *can* know and *name* your secret, *and* be close *enough* to hurt you or blackmail you with it.

The neighbor is *that* who you have made *sure* that your *private issues* have *remained* private, during all these late night arguments, sex session, and long shower songs...

The neighbor is that who *knows* you have sex, but should not *hear* it.

The *value of your privacy* vis-à-vis the neighbor, is *higher*.

The neighbor is that *first* profile that pops up on Grindr (Gay sex Application), due to the *closeness* of the location. It is also the *first* profile that the Arab queer *blocks:*

Fear of the queer neighbor.

Inversely, the neighbor is *that* who the Arab queer wants to find the *most* on Grindr. *That* who the queer *wants* to hold a secret *against*, for reasons of protection and cautiousness, incase that neighbor ever found any "queer secrets" on *them.*

It is a war of secrets, and the "Queer secret" takes the win, giving the *discloser/ exposer* arsenal *against* the *disclosed/ exposed.* The neighbor symbolizes *to* the Arab queer that *close* subject it desperately wants to touch and consume, and *almost* can, but *cannot.* The relationship between the Arab queer and the neighbor is a voyeuristic, fetishized relationship based on simultaneous *insecure attachment* and *aversion.* It is metaphoric of the relationship of the queer *towards* himself *and* the relationship of Arab culture *towards* the queer.

166

"Sometimes I wait outside my window for hours to see Ayman (local grocery store owner). He calls me "ya helou" (handsome) every morning. I am sure that "Khaso"[xxxiv]. He can't see me see him because it would be disastrous. He would set the men of the neighborhood on me if he knew I was queer. They are very religious you know, but most of them "khason 3al sikeit " (are silently involved)"

– Salim, 19, Lebanese

Salim's carnal instinct made him get up and wait by the windowsill... *Wait*, but *not* approach...Wanting *and* fearing. This "neighborly" relationship appears to be contradictory in nature, while some might see it as complementary, even *necessary* for the maintenance of queer Arab *pleasure*.

According to research, the general approach to *insecure attachments*, namely the Arab queer's attachement *to* his or her neighbor, has *one* of *two* reactions: The first reaction is *attachment anxiety* referring to the feelings of rejection and abandonment while simultaneously yearning for excessive *closeness*.

The second reaction is *avoidance anxiety* that refers to the *withdrawal* from intimacy and dependency,

Both results produce an anxious queer phallus.

xxxiv "Khasso" is often used in colloquial Lebanese Queer Language insinuating an individual's involvement in queer events. The term translates to English as "involved". The term also distinguishes itself from the term "gay" and shows the fear of using queer terms in public. "Khaso?" is part of a secret queer language that if heard by an Arab heterosexual, would not be understood as "involved in Queerness". This is how Arab queers maneuver in fear and anxiety around heterosexual norms in order to identify queerness in a specific environment.

The queer's relationship to the neighbor is important because *this* form of a "relation-ing" is the strongest and longest form of *attachement formation* the queer experiences.

This is how an Arab queer *knows* how to attach: Insecurely, anxiously and at a distance. This *social imprint* of "relation-ing" goes on to depict the *future* relationship of the queer to itself and to others.

Arab queers that grow in a lacking of care and from *the neighbor* experience *attachment insecurity,* which manifests differently in Western and non-Western cultures (Harma & Sumar, 2015).

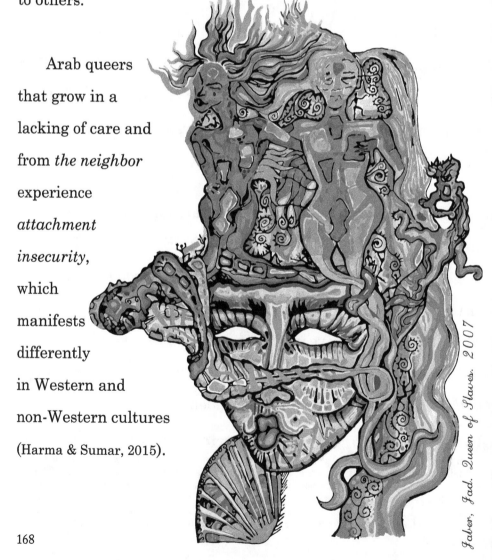

Jaber, Fad. Queen of Slaves. 2007

Attachment insecurity is manifested *more* violently in *collective* cultures where queer attachment/ *closeness* is not allowed or outwardly encouraged, yet is tailored into the fabric of *being* Arab and into the gendered, spatial and cultural configurations. Attachment insecurity increases the symptoms of *attachment anxiety* within the queer subject towards *the neighbor* namely "the other", towards *society* namely "the big other", and towards *the self*.

BEING QUEER MAKES *EVERYONE* YOUR "NEIGHBOR".

Faber, Jad. The Heightened Ego. 2010

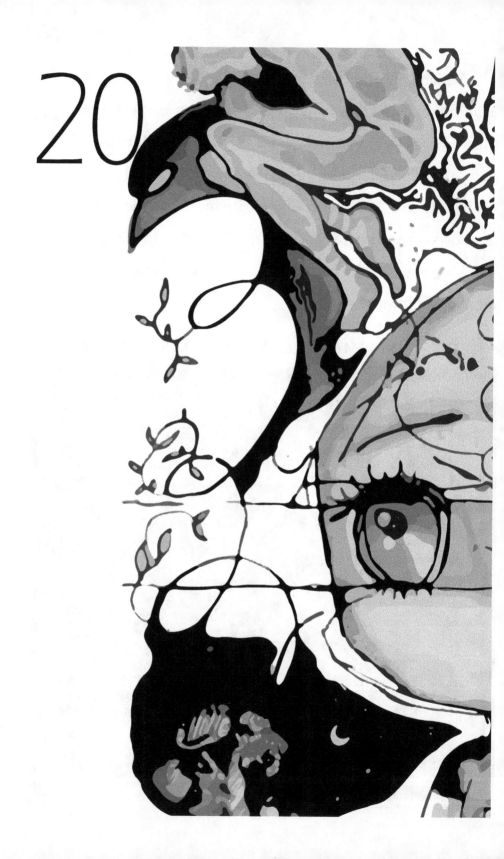

No Queer
Is an Island

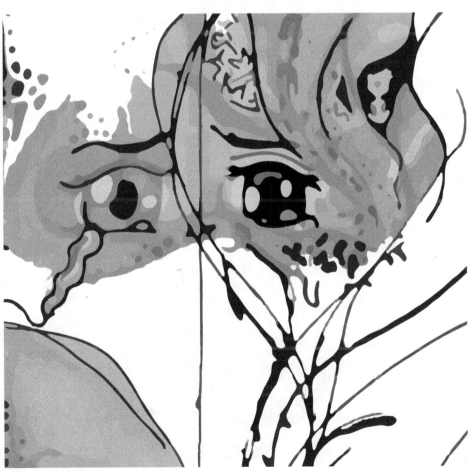

CHAPTER TWENTY

No Queer Is an Island

Being queer *and* Arab neighbors the world around you. It creates a conflicted relationship with *all* the involved social stakeholders: the *closer* the queer to the neighbor, the *more* the chance of conflict over one's queer choices. For example, the mother is the *closest* neighbor to the Arab queer. Arab queers generally conflict with their mothers *first* over their identity formation. They also fear *the mother*'s trespass into their queer lives, more so than any other *neighbor*.It is time that the queer asserts closeness, and *not* distance, as they come out unto their queer self. It is time that they negotiate neither their *closeness*, nor their queerness.

Being Arab entails a certain level of closeness that is part of *all* the social rituals[xxxv], norms[xxxvi] and spaces[xxxvii]. For Western cultures extreme closeness and clinging to the partner are seen as a source of relationship dissatisfaction (Goodwin, Rothbaum) and maturing into an adult and independent self entails severing from that level of familial closeness[xxxviii].

In contrast, extreme closeness is highly desired by couples in collectivist cultures like Lebanon, GCC countries, and Japan. Closeness is not seen as abnormal or maladaptive and personal harmony is contingent upon an excessive need for care from others. Arab queers *want* and *desire* to be *close* to their *culture*, as they have been *acculturated* into it. But they are also forced to desire anonymity when experiencing anything outside the framework of the heteronormative archetype, because being queer compromises their closeness to people around them.

xxxv   Funeral and wedding rituals are extremely expansive usually involving the entire village or locality, They last up to three months, throughout which the bereaved are visited daily, given lunch and dinner, medically assisted etc. This is a testament to the level of *closeness* shared in Arab culture during events of death, sickness and trauma

xxxvi   Arab girls and their fathers, as well as Arab boys and their mothers, have a very *close* physical and emotional relationship. It is quite normal to see Arab men in their forties kiss and be kissed by their mothers fervently. It is *as* common to see mothers sending Arab men their daily favorite meal, outside their wife's cooking, even after they have been married for more than three years*. This is an example of the constant attempts of the Arab man's mother to influence *his* household further, and is infamously known in Arab culture as the conflicted relationship of "the *Kinni* and the *Hamat*": Arabic for "the wife and the mother-in-law". This cultural concept is highly represented on local Television shows in the Gulf, Lebanon, Syria and Jordan.

xxxvii   Arab adults stay home until they are married and come back home after divorce. They remain close to their family home before, during and after marriage.

xxxviii   In the US, as a right of passage into adulthood, young men and women at the age of eighteen are meant to leave their homes and "find their own way".

The particular condition of the Arab queer makes him or her *worth* the special attention in this modern queer struggle. The possibility of drawing comparisons between minority queer Arab culture and other minority queer cultures in global contexts should be of interest to social theorists, especially with *more* people identifying as queer rather than normative, as part of an *androgynous* and gender-fluid global culture.

Can we draw comparisons between a closeted lesbian woman living in the Bronx and a closeted homosexual man in Saudi Arabia? By bringing together queer language and thought from diverse academics, we just might. For the dogmatic Arab society, this book provides a philosophy and language, *not* to provide answers, but to ask question, but not the *wrong* questions... The *wrong* questions are what we call ideology:

"ARE YOU READY TO LIVE WITHOUT A FAMILY?"

"WHY ARE YOU NOT MARRIED AT 30? WHAT IS WRONG WITH YOU?"

"DID YOU HAVE A BAD CHILDHOOD?"

When asking *these* questions, language is forcibly taking the queer back to a *heteronormative* reply, *away* from questions that give queer Arab agency and subjectivity a *new* light and a feeling of well roundedness that *deserves* admission and representation.

Similar to asking the prisoner "How does the warden treat you", who almost *always* replies with "very well", *versus* asking the prisoner "how do *you* like to be treated". The Arab queer *is* confined within Arab culture, awaiting *the revolution* that might be *prompted* with a few *queer* questions.

The decisive question for the queer is: Is it related to something *infinite* or not? (Jung, 1964) Spirituality and enlightenment are born of suffering and the Arab queer has suffered *enough*: This queer lotus has been born from the mud of heteronormative Arab culture.

"DO YOU HOPE FOR MARRIAGE
EQUALITY IN LEBANON?"

"DO YOU HOPE TO ADOPT KIDS AS
A QUEER COUPLE IN THE FUTURE?"

"HOW WOULD
YOU DEFINE YOUR
EXPERIENCE OF QUEER
LOVE?"

"TELL ME YOUR
QUEEREST DREAMS..."

Jaber, Jad. The Bigger Questions. 2010

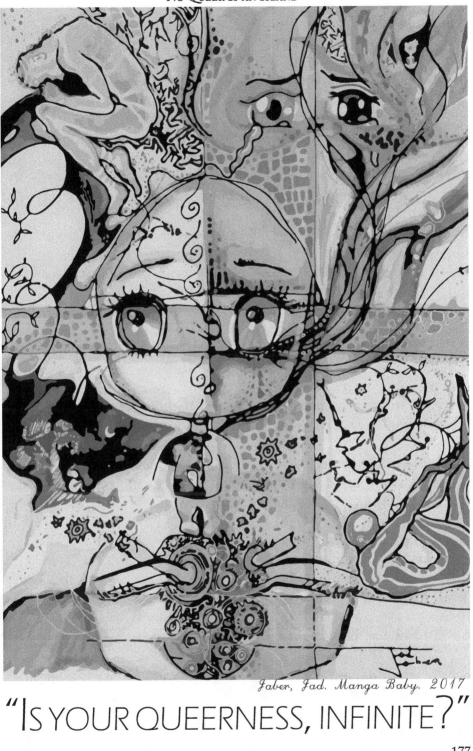

Jaber, Jad. Manga Baby. 2017

"IS YOUR QUEERNESS, INFINITE?"

BIBLIOGRAPHY:

Badiou, Alain. "The Event in Deleuze." *PARRHESIA* 2 (2007): 37.

Foucault, Michel. *The History of Sexuality.* New York: Pantheon Books, 1990.

Friedman, R. Z. "Kant and Kierkegaard: The limits of reason and the cunning of faith." International journal for philosophy of religion 19, no. 1 (1986): 3-22.

Grosz, Barbara J., and Candace L. Sidner. "Attention, intentions, and the structure of discourse." *Computational linguistics* 12, no. 3 (1986): 175-204.

CG Jung ,RFC Hull, trans., The collected works of CG Jung, 1961; CW 4; par. 665.

CG Jung. " *Memories, Dreams, Reflections",* 1963, Vintage Books, p.3.

Kant, Immanuel. "On External Objects." *In Critique of Pure Reason* , by Immanuel Kant, 1, 1781.

Kant, Immanuel, and Paul Guyer. Critique of pure reason. London: Cambridge University Press, 1998.

Mehmet Harma & Nebi Sümer (2015): Are avoidant wives and anxious husbands unhappy in a collectivist context? Dyadic associations in established marriages, Journal of Family Studies, 2015.

Michael W. Morris, Kwok Leung, Daniel Ames and Brian Lickel. " Views from inside and outside: Integrating Emic and Etic Insights about Culture and Justice Judgment." *The Academy of Management Review* 24, no. 4 (October 1999): 781-796.

Nietzsche, Friedrich. —. *Thus Spoke Zarathustra A Book for All and None* . Edited by Adrien Del Caro and Robert B. Pippin. Translated by Adrien Del Caro. New York: Cambridge University press, 2006.

Presse, Agence France. "dailystar.com.lb." *DailyStar.com.* August 11, 2011. www.dailystar.com.lb> News> Aug-11 (accessed August 17, 2010).

O'Rourke, Michael, "The Big Secret About Queer Theory", A Journal of Queer Studies
#9 (2014)

Potter, Claire, "Queer Hoover: Sex, Lies, and Political History" (2006). Division II Faculty Publications, Paper 21.

Sartre, Jean-Paul. The transcendence of the ego: An existentialist theory of consciousness. Vol. 114. *: Macmillan, 1957.

Secomb, Linell. Philosophy and Love: From plato to Popular culture. Edinburgh: Edinburgh University Press, 2007Ed.

Zizek, Slavoj. *Enjoy your symptom!: Jacques Lacan in Hollywood and out.* *: Routledge, 2013.

Zizek, Slavoj. "The Structure of Domination Today: A Lacanian View." *Studies in East European Thought* 56, no. 4 (2004): 383-403.